THE BATTLE OF WAYNESBORO

RICHARD G. WILLIAMS JR.

The History Press

Published by The History Press
Charleston, SC 29403
www.historypress.net

First published 2014

ISBN 978.1.5402.0855.2

Library of Congress CIP data applied for.

Dedicated to Guy Williams, the man who instilled in me an interest in the War Between the States, pride in my southern heritage and a love of grits. Thanks, Dad.

CONTENTS

ACKNOWLEDGEMENTS

I am profusely grateful for the eagerness and generosity of all those who assisted me in writing this account of the Battle of Waynesboro. Heretofore, there have been no books written specifically about this battle. As is fitting, the impetus and motivation for taking on such a project, along with the research it would require, came from many of Waynesboro's own. That, of course, deserves acknowledgement and gratitude. Shirley Bridgeforth, who serves as president of the Waynesboro Heritage Foundation (WHF), was invaluable in her encouragement and assistance in helping me gather the research for such an endeavor. Shirley's enthusiasm for "Waynesborough's" history is infectious. The very existence of the WHF would not be possible without her tireless dedication in preserving the history of this community. Karen Church assisted with images and other research questions. Her volunteer work for WHF makes these often overlooked and underfunded community efforts toward preserving local history possible. Karen Vest, archivist for the Waynesboro Public Library, also provided much assistance with obtaining images and directing me to additional resources.

Mary Highsmith, who is related to the Withrow family, provided much-needed material and answered questions about that family's patriarch, Colonel C.H. Withrow. Mary's research helped answer some questions regarding the relationship between my great-grandfather and Colonel Withrow. John Plumb was kind enough to allow me to use his research on his ancestral home, the Plumb House. John Huffer, longtime Waynesboro resident and relic hunter/preserver extraordinaire, has done the community an immense favor in preserving and sharing his vast collection of area artifacts with the public. Local historian and author George Hawke was most gracious in allowing me to use his unpublished research on Hugh Lafferty Gallaher. And, once again, fellow Shenandoah Valley native and historian Robert Moore provided an invaluable critique, insight and assistance in clarifying certain questions about regiments and specifics surrounding the battle, as well as recommended sources and offering suggestions to improve the manuscript.

Longtime friend Douglas Hill also provided encouragement and research assistance. Another local historian and expert on the history of Fishburne Military School, J.B. Yount, was kind enough to spend some time chatting with me about questions regarding James Abbott Fishburne. And I am grateful to Dr. Anita Henderson for sharing her knowledge and research regarding Maria Lewis's possible involvement in the Battle of Waynesboro.

Thanks to Banks Smither and the good folks at The History Press for numerous deadline extensions. All of the people at The History Press have been a pleasure to work with. As always, my wife's patience with those delays and for putting up with my oft-repeated, "If I just had one more week," deserves more than just thanks. Lastly, thanks to my God for allowing me to complete something very near and dear to my family and what I hope and pray will benefit my hometown as we commemorate the sesquicentennial of the Battle of Waynesboro.

In the winter of '65,
we were hungry, just barely alive.
By May the 10th, Richmond had fell,
it's a time I remember, oh so well.
                                    —Robbie Robertson

INTRODUCTION

The lines are fallen unto me in pleasant places; yea, I have a goodly heritage.
—Psalms 16:6

Sitting in my basement office typing the manuscript to this book, I am surrounded by mementos that constantly remind me of my hometown of Waynesboro, Virginia. Among them is an old photograph of Confederate veteran and former mayor of Waynesboro Colonel Charles H. Withrow. And there's the bridle bit that belonged to Withrow's horse, "Bird," hanging on the wall. There's also a portrait of my great-grandfather, "Mr. Charlie" McGann, who cared for the Colonel's horse in the early part of the twentieth century. There's the antique, wood-framed barber's mirror that used to adorn a barbershop in Waynesboro's African American community on Port Republic Road. Just up the road from that barbershop was the elementary school that I attended after desegregation in the 1960s—the Rosenwald School. These items, along with many others, are old friends that summon up misty-sweet memories.

I grew up in a Waynesboro neighborhood known as Wayne Hills, just a few blocks west of Port Republic Road. In early March 1865, that area would have witnessed Confederate artillery shells sailing overhead as Confederate artillerist Henry Robinson Berkeley fired his cannon at Sheridan's advancing army from the high ground near Port Republic Road. Just a bike ride across town lived my paternal grandparents. As a young boy, I visited my grandparents often and spent many restless summer nights lying in a bed in a second-story bedroom of their home. I recall the air often being still and humid, and I would move my pillow to the bottom of the bed, getting closer to the open window in the hopes of catching a breeze of relief. The summer sounds—crickets and cicadas and the occasional barking of a dog—filled the night air. Charles Lockridge McGann started building the home in 1909 on the corner of what was Locust Avenue and Fourth (now Fourteenth) Street. Downstairs, hanging on an archway that joined a hallway to the dining room, was my great-great grandfather's Civil War musket.

The sounds I would hear on those summer nights were much more serene than the ones that filled the air in March 1865. The McGann home sat squarely in the middle of ground that had hosted the Battle of Waynesboro—the last Civil War battle fought in the Shenandoah Valley, on March 2, 1865. The home was built in an area that would later become known as the "Tree Streets"—designated a historic district and listed on the National Register of Historic Places in 2002; it is a 120-acre area of stately, late nineteenth- and early twentieth-century homes and structures. During the American colonial and Victorian periods, it was common practice to name streets running north to south after American species of trees. As the old battlefield reverted to farmland after the war, it became part of an apple orchard and was then developed into a quintessential southern residential neighborhood with Victorian-style homes lining the streets of Oak, Cherry, Locust, Pine, Maple, Walnut and Chestnut Avenues. Included in part of the Tree Street historic district is Wayne Avenue, named in honor of the town's namesake: Revolutionary War general "Mad Anthony" Wayne.

From that bedroom in my grandparents' home, hands folded under my chin on my pillow, I could look out the second-story window up the hill one block away toward Pine Avenue and what had been the Confederate line—the very line where my great-great-grandfather's unit, the 51st Virginia Infantry, had dug trenches in what would prove to be a futile attempt to repel Union general Philip Sheridan's numerically superior army.

And there were other memories: stories and objects that would sometimes sweep a young boy's imagination into the time warp that William Faulkner described in *Intruder in the Dust*:

> *For every Southern boy fourteen years old, not once but whenever he wants it, there is the instant when it's still not yet two o'clock on that July afternoon in 1863, the brigades are in position behind the rail fence, the guns are laid and ready in the woods and the furled flags are already loosened to break out and Pickett himself with his long oiled ringlets and his hat in one*

John McGann (on right) and his wife, Mary, standing next to young girl. Taken in Nelson County at the McGann homeplace, circa 1900–1910. *Author's collection.*

hand probably and his sword in the other looking up the hill waiting for Longstreet to give the word and it's all in the balance, it hasn't happened yet, it hasn't even begun yet, it not only hasn't begun yet but there is still time for it not to begin against that position and those circumstances which made more men than Garnett and Kemper and Armistead and Wilcox look grave yet it's going to begin, we all know that, we have come too far with too much at stake and that moment doesn't need even a fourteen-year-old boy to think This time. Maybe this time *with all this much to lose and all this much to gain: Pennsylvania, Maryland, the world, the golden dome of Washington itself to crown with desperate and unbelievable victory the desperate gamble, the cast made two years ago.*

In writing those words, Faulkner seemed to be manifesting what Ernest Hemingway described as the task of writing: "There is nothing to writing. All you do is sit down at a typewriter and bleed." And when one writes about wars and battles, one *must* bleed—at least metaphorically. For wars and battles are about much more than glory and gain, more than conquerors and conquered, more than troop movements and maneuvers—wars and battles are about bleeding, about the loss of life, about what was won and what might have been won, what might have been prevented, what might have been saved or lost. It is impossible to read the letters, diaries and accounts of battles without, at least to some degree, entering into what the writer of those accounts was feeling and describing. To do less would be a disservice to all those who bled and died in those battles.

Yet historians and writers are advised to separate their own emotions and feelings from their work. But is that really possible? It is even advisable? Of course writers should, as much as possible, restrain their biases when presenting history. But what is writing without emotion? What is storytelling without sharing the passion of the event? Stale facts and recounting of numbers killed and wounded do not tell the story adequately. While connections to subjects and events can be a stumbling block when attempting to write objectively about those same topics, they can also serve as motivations—even giving keen insight and unique perspective attainable no other way. It certainly motivates me. And it is no coincidence that the biographers of the South's two greatest Civil War generals were themselves southerners.

The definitive biography of Thomas "Stonewall" Jackson was authored by historian James I. Robertson Jr., who has said that he developed a keen interest in Civil War studies when he first became aware that his great-grandfather had been a Confederate soldier and cook for Robert E. Lee.

And Robert E. Lee's most noted biographer, Douglas Southall Freeman, penned his massive four-volume biography of Lee due to a personal attachment to the War Between the States and after being "profoundly moved" by something he had witnessed. Freeman biographer David Johnson gives some of the details of what Freeman experienced when, as a seventeen-year-old young man, he observed a reenactment of the Battle of the Crater:

> *Douglas stood with his Confederate veteran father and watched the pageant of history unfold in front of him. Back at the hotel, he saw the veterans from a closer vantage point. They were "feeble, crippled, some of them blind, many of them poor." He was profoundly moved by the events of the day…All these emotions, shaped and colored by his heritage as a son of the South and Walker Freeman, had evoked self-examination and prompted action. Now, he made to himself a solemn commitment, one that he knew would outlast the zeal of youthful novelties.*
>
> *"If someone doesn't write the story of these men," Douglas Southall Freeman resolved, "it will be lost forever."*
>
> *"I'm going to do it."*[1]

Some historians have even grieved over the fact that they *lack* such a connection as Robertson and Freeman:

> *Any historian who argues that the Confederate people demonstrated robust devotion to their slave-based republic, possessed feelings of national community, and sacrificed more than any other segment of white society in United States history runs the risk of being labeled a neo-Confederate. As a native of Los Angeles who grew up on a farm in southern Colorado, I can claim complete freedom from any pro-Confederate special pleading during my formative years. Moreover, not a single ancestor fought in the war, a fact I lamented as a boy reading books by Bruce Catton and Douglas Southall Freeman and wanting desperately to have some direct connection to the events that fascinated me.*[2]

Both Robertson and Freeman have been criticized by other Civil War scholars and historians for being "too close" to their subjects. That is a fair observation and one, I believe, neither man would have totally denied. But knowing these historians' "closeness" to their subjects and the widely acclaimed quality of their scholarship, did this closeness really detract from their work—or did it actually enhance it? Gary Gallagher, in his introduction to the 1998 edition of Freeman's *The South to Posterity*, seems to echo that sentiment in quoting Bruce Catton: "[It] would be foolish to pretend that Dr. Freeman's history was at all times completely objective. It was scholarly and it was fair, but it was never detached or passionless. It would be poorer history if it were those things."[3]

It is my opinion that readers should be much more skeptical of historians and writers who refuse to acknowledge their biases and connections to the topics they write about, as well as of those writers who, though admitting their biases, make no attempt to bridle them.

The Battle of Waynesboro, along with the rich heritage and history of the whole Shenandoah Valley, is part of me, and I want readers to know this. As historian Jeffrey Wert has astutely observed, the Shenandoah Valley has an almost spiritual connection with its residents, particularly those who are native to its soil: "In the Shenandoah Valley of Virginia, roots went deep into the rich soil…The Valley seeped into bones, touched souls."[4]

So, as you read *The Battle of Waynesboro*, know that the author was born on and grew up on the very ground that hosted the conflict. Know that all six of my children were born on that battlefield. Know that I have never lived more than ten miles from that ground. Know that two of my great-great-grandfathers served in the 51st Virginia Infantry, which fought in that battle. Know that my family and I have owned some of that battleground. Know that I have held swords, bullets, grapeshot and a musket from that battle. Know that my body has been nourished from food grown from that ground. Know that I reverence that ground, that connection and that heritage. Know that this ground has seeped into my bones and touched my soul. Know that all this simultaneously burdens and rewards me with certain biases and perspectives. Know also that while I have attempted to bridle my biases, I am, at the same time, thankful to God for the heritage that birthed them. And finally, know that I have sat at my keyboard and bled a little.

RICHARD G. WILLIAMS JR.
Huckleberry Hollow, Virginia
July 2014

Chapter 1

In the Shadow of the Blue Ridge

There may be a lovelier country somewhere—in the Island Vale of Avalon, at a gamble—but when the sunlight lies upon it and the wind puts white clouds racing their shadows the Shenandoah Valley is as good as anything America can show.
—Bruce Catton

A book about the Battle of Waynesboro would be incomplete without some insight into the history and background of the town, as well as a look at a few of the individuals from Waynesboro who offered their services for the Confederate cause.

Waynesboro, Virginia, is located at the eastern edge of Augusta County in the central Shenandoah Valley and at the foot of Afton Mountain, in the shadow of the Blue Ridge Mountains—the eastern range of the Appalachians. It was, at the time of the Civil War, the second-largest town (behind Staunton) in Augusta County. Like so many early settlements in America, it is located on the banks of a river. In George R. Hawke's two-volume history of Waynesboro, he noted:

> *The beginnings of Waynesboro formed where the trail from Rockfish Gap to Staunton (originally Beverley's Mill Place, then Augusta Court House) crossed the South River [Southern Fork of the Shenandoah River] at a shallow gravelly ford. The original crossing may have been in the vicinity of the present Main Street bridge, or upstream from there, possibly as far as Club Court hairpin curve near Lovers Lane. The 1400-*

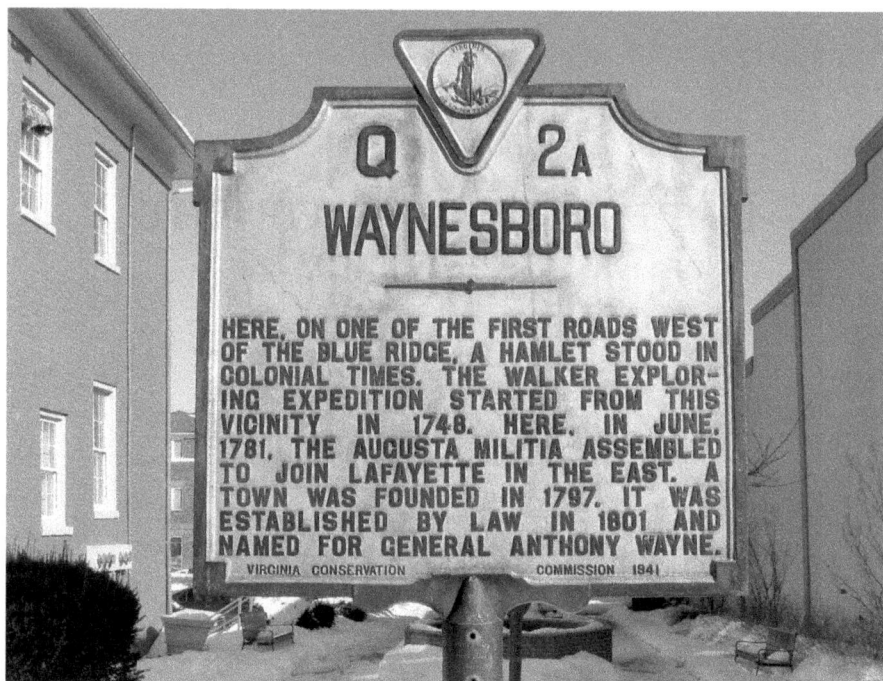

Virginia Historical Highway Marker. Main Street, Waynesboro, Virginia. *Photo by author.*

*foot altitude assured moderate summer temperatures. Springs, timber and
tillable soil were nearby, and a north–south trail crossed the east–west one
near the Stuart/Pratt home. Local deposits of iron, manganese, copper
and porcelain clay were found in profitable amounts. Finally, Waynesboro
built on a foundation of good people—the early settlers were capable, God
fearing and hard working.*[5]

Before the town was officially called "Waynesborough," it was referred to
in diaries, letters and by locals as "Teesville" or "Teasville." That name was
apparently derived from the fact that there was a tavern or inn known as the Teas
Place, Teas Tavern and the Widow Teas. Joseph Teas had purchased 465 acres
from the Beverly Patent[6] in 1739. He purchased additional land before his death
in 1755. That additional acreage would become known as Teasville and, later,
Waynesborough. It was actually Joseph Teas's daughter-in-law, Mary Reid Teas,
who began operating her home as an inn after the death of her husband (and son
of Joseph Teas), William. Several sources note that George Washington, Thomas
Jefferson and French officer Major General Marquis de Chastellux all stayed

at the Widow Teas's Inn. After lodging at Jefferson's Monticello, De Chastellux would later write that the inn was, as Jefferson had warned him, "one of the worst in America."[7]

Officially laid out in 1797, the Virginia General Assembly approved the request for a charter of Waynesborough as a town in 1801. Although some sources suggest that the town was named for Revolutionary War hero General "Mad Anthony" Wayne's victory over Indians, fought on the banks of the South River at Teasville, there is no record of any such battle taking place there. It is more likely that the settlement became the namesake of the war hero due to the fact that Joseph Teas's granddaughter, Jane Teas Estill, admired General Wayne and suggested that the town adopt it.

In addition to the South River, the area also boasted several bold springs, which further encouraged settlement. The springs and wells they supported provided water for animals and travelers using the well-worn road that connected Staunton (to the west) and Charlottesville (to the east) and also served as the town's main thoroughfare. Despite the convenient location and

Top: Rob Langdon of Albemarle County, Virginia, found this seventeenth-century button on the banks of the South River near Waynesboro—a silent witness to the area's long history. *Used by permission.*

Bottom: General Anthony Wayne, published by Whitney McDermut & Company, circa 1878. *Courtesy Library of Congress.*

19

abundant water supply, the 1810 census showed only 250 residents. By the outbreak of the Civil War, the town had only seen an addition of some 200 more souls, making the total population 457.

But before the Battle of Waynesboro came to the small community in 1865, Waynesboro sent its own soldiers to fight for the Confederacy in April 1861. Despite its small population, the town of Waynesboro (also sometimes spelled "Waynesborough" at the time of the Civil War) and other areas of eastern Augusta County managed to raise a company of volunteers to fight for the Confederacy. First known as the "Valley Rangers," the unit later became Company E of the 1st Virginia Cavalry. Although the company included men from the eastern part of Augusta County, it was one of only two companies fully organized and recognized as being from Waynesboro.[8] The Valley Rangers unit was first organized in 1859 and mustered in at New Hope, just a few miles north of Waynesboro. The motivation for the formation of this militia unit was typical for much of the South. The looming war clouds on the horizon—while worrisome and foreboding to some—inspired patriotism and "much military enthusiasm" among many a southern boy and young man. Anxious for glory and adventure, these men were eager to associate with a military unit. Such was the case for a good number of volunteers in the Valley Rangers.

As part of the 1st Virginia Cavalry, Company E would be involved at and distinguish itself in a number of locations and battles, including Brandy Station, Gettysburg, Yellow Tavern, Cold Harbor, Winchester, Waynesboro and Appomattox, to name a few. All totaled, the 1st Virginia Cavalry fought in more than two hundred engagements, and a number of distinguished Confederate officers were associated with this regiment: J.E.B. Stuart, John Singleton Mosby, William E. "Grumble"

Sergeant B.F. Smith of Company B, 52nd Virginia Infantry Regiment, and Company F, 1st Virginia Cavalry Regiment, circa 1861–65. *Courtesy Library of Congress.*

The Waynesboro Academy. *Courtesy Waynesboro Heritage Museum.*

Jones and Fitzhugh Lee. The most detailed—romanticized as it is—account of the mustering of the Valley Rangers as the company prepared to march off to fight for the Confederacy was penned by one of its own members, Elliott Guthrie Fishburne, who enlisted as a private and would eventually attain the rank of third sergeant. This account, titled "Reminiscences" and part of an article titled "Early Civil War Days in Waynesboro," was published by the Augusta County Historical Society in 1974.[9] The exact date of the original account is not known. But in introducing the account, Fishburne noted that it was "[w]ritten by request for a young lady who read it at a meeting of the 'Daughters of the Confederacy'—in Waynesboro, Va., March 1897." Fishburne described the pageantry of that memorable day as he and other local boys gathered in front of the old Waynesboro Academy on April 19, 1861, to march off to defend their homes and firesides:

> *What a thrilling time it was in that Spring of 1861 "when a Nation was born" and a most glorious chapter in human bearing and daring was written. When the Southern Confederacy, that inspiration of Cavaliers and Righteousness, that inspirer of heroes, who pricked their names on the pages of history with sword and bayonet point, of Poets who "wreathed around*

with glory" the Southern Cross, of Matrons and Maidens who gave more than life to its defence [sic]. Then began the assemblying of that Southern Manhood and boyhood who were to go "Sounding down the ages" as the Confederate Army. Among the first to enroll themselves under its banner were "The Valley Rangers"—a volunteer cavalry company—composed of the very best of the young men living along the Eastern side of Augusta County, who under their first Captain—the brave Patrick—(who later as Major of the 17th Battalion was to die gloriously on the plains of Second Manassas) met in historic Waynesboro to go to the front. 'Twas when the comedy parts in the great opening drama commenced. How exercised we were about our uniforms, how we had to send off for the material, and get just the right shade of color—and the exact buttons, braid, etc.! How we watched the making of them and how impatient we got—and at length—when finished, and donned, how we did strut and how gorgeous we were with our wide yellow (the cavalry color) striped trousers and braided coats and bright, brass buttons (a gross of them more or less) and our hats, great, widebrimmed slouches, with plume and gilt cord and tassel, and what a sight was the little fellow in his over large clothes. My Eye! but it was comic; and our pictures would grace the Sunday newspaper of today. Then, at last, when everything was ready—our horses, the finest and best in the county, groomed to perfection, with plaited manes and tales, new saddles with bright red blankets and girths, our big, old fashioned saddlepockets stuffed to bulging with every useful article—etc., enough for an army in later days. And the joke of it all was that not one in ten had a weapon of any kind, unless it was a toy pistol or so, and to think of such a going to war!

But then, the guns we would (and did) get later—from the enemy! How vividly the scene comes back of our last mustering. How we formed in the Main Street—and as we mounted

Elliott G. Fishburne. *Courtesy University of Virginia Library.*

our horses for the last time—of the motherly caress and cautions—the fathers' advice—the sisters' proud smile and the admiring looks of the younger brothers and the servants— and then, the sly embrace of the sweetheart behind the parlor door, when we rushed in to say good by for the twentieth time! Last came the presentation of our flag and farewell address of our good and true old Parson Richardson. Then from our Captain came "Attention Company!" "By twos March!" "Head of Column right!" And away we marched for Harper's Ferry to fight Yankees and without a gun. (Pure comedy that—with no

Major William Patrick. *Courtesy Waynesboro Public Library.*

chance for a tragedy). What an enjoyable march it was. To us boys, it was as when school closed—and we reveled in the sense of freedom and dreamed of the great and daring deeds we would perform. The march down the Valley that lovely April was enjoyed ever so much. How we laughed and chatted by the way and now and then tried the speed and mettle of our horses and how we were cheered and admired by the girls all along the route. And the great event, our arrival at Harper's Ferry, where was forming that grand army that later—as the Army of Northern Virginia.[10]

The "brave Patrick" to whom Fishburne refers was William Patrick, whose family was part of the Scotch-Irish migration from Pennsylvania down the Great Wagon Road into the Shenandoah Valley. Patrick's great-grandfather and namesake fought in the Revolutionary War. William Patrick became a prominent leader in and around Waynesboro, serving as the sheriff of Augusta County. Enlisting in Company E of the 1st Virginia Cavalry, Patrick was made captain and would later be promoted to major in June 1862 for "bravery on the field."[11] After dying on September 2, 1862, from wounds received during the battle of Second Manassas, Stonewall Jackson would write of Patrick, "He fell in the attack while setting an example of gallantry to his men well worthy of imitation." And Jeb Stuart would add, "He lived long enough to witness the triumph of our arms and expired thus in the arms of victory. The sacrifice was noble, but the loss was irreparable."[12] He is buried in the Patrick family cemetery at his ancestral home, Locust Isle, north of Waynesboro. The epitaph on his headstone reads, "A brave and noble soldier and true patriot."

Although Fishburne's account would appear to indicate that locals were eager for war, that was not the case. Waynesboro, along with surrounding Augusta County, was solidly pro-Union when the Virginia Convention voted on April 4, 1861, with all but four of the fifteen Shenandoah Valley delegates to the convention voting against secession. Despite local opposition to secession, once Virginia voted to secede, Waynesboro would offer its best

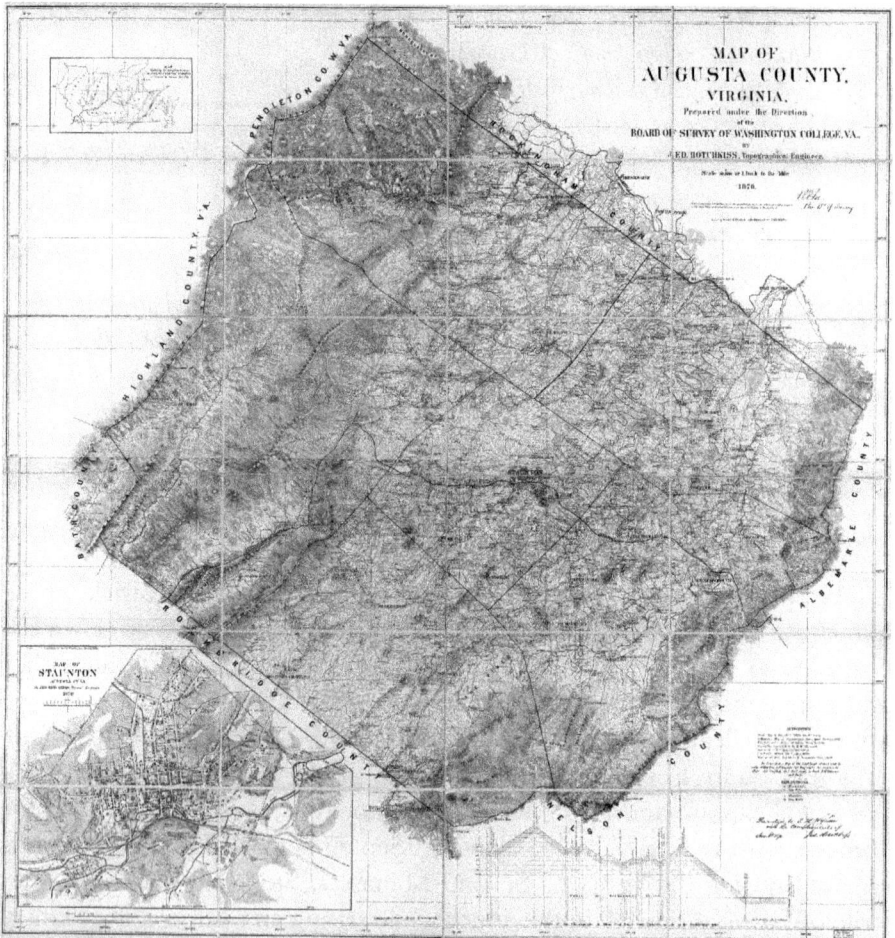

Map of Augusta County by Jedediah Hotchkiss, 1870. The basis of this map is the Confederate surveys made by order of Major General J.F. Gilmer during the War Between the States. *Courtesy Library of Congress.*

for the cause. Of course, the boys from Waynesboro were not the only Shenandoah Valley soldiers marching into Harper's Ferry. As historian Jeffrey Wert noted:

> *In the days that ensued* [after Virginia's secession] *additional companies of Valley men arrived at Harper's Ferry. The units bore names such as the West Augusta Guards, Augusta Rifles, Rockbridge Rifles, Staunton Artillery, Southern Guards, and Mountain Guards. Each company had its own "uniform"—the Mountain Guards wore red flannel shirts and gray trousers; the West Augusta Guards and Augusta Rifles, gray woolen jackets and trousers; and the Southern Guards, blue flannel shirts, gray trousers, and United States Navy caps. One company carried a flag given to it while en route from women in Harrisonburg* [13]

Elliott Fishburne also shared some of his experiences and observations after arriving at Harper's Ferry, as well as some memories of battle experiences:

View of Harper's Ferry, Virginia, 1860. *Courtesy Library of Congress.*

Pretty soon our camp at the Ferry was broken up and the war began in earnest. Then our Company, now known as Company E, 1ˢᵗ Virginia Cavalry, made the first fight in the valley by a skirmish with a lot of Yankees across the Potomac at Williamsport—and in a few days we had our first man shot (Gam Dalhouse) and then we fought along with the West August Guards of Staunton and the Rockbridge Artillery and the other troops under Jackson (the building Stonewall brigade) at "Falling Waters" and under J.E.B. Stuart our Major and then and afterwards our Great Cavalry General. We captured the very first company of Yankees—and had one of our company (Zach Johnson) wounded. Both Johnson and Dalhouse died in a few months—partly from their wounds.

It was in this fight at Falling Waters that Major D.W. Drake and Capt. John Opie—then privates in the West Augusta Guards—being a little in advance of our line of battle and so intent on firing at the Yankees—did not notice the withdrawal of their command—but continued shooting—and thus, those two brave boys held in check the Yankee General Patterson's army—for a while, and then fell back in good order without a scratch. Both of these boys afterwards performed many deeds of bravery but the holding in check of an Army was great. But it was not all tragedy. As when the fight was fun—and there we got the variety—tragedy and comedy that was the spice of our soldier life. [14]

Part of the "spice" of a soldier's life was receiving something from home—a rare treat for a Confederate soldier. Fishburne described that experience:

O! those boxes from home! What delights they were both in giving and receiving! How carefully were their contents selected. The best of everything at home was for the soldier boys. And then, how the boys enjoyed them; and how unselfish they were, calling in all their friends to the feast. [15]

Other soldiers from Waynesboro also provided some insight into a Civil War soldier's life and experiences. Perhaps the best-recorded experiences by any member of Company E of the 1ˢᵗ Virginia Cavalry (Valley Rangers) from Waynesboro are those of the Gallaher (pronounced "gal-yer") brothers DeWitt Clinton and William Bowen. Both men were born at Shepherdstown, Virginia (today, West Virginia). Their father was Hugh Lafferty Gallaher. He was originally from Lebanon, Pennsylvania, before moving to Shepherdstown, where he met and married Elizabeth Bowen. The elder Gallaher worked as a contractor building railroads,[16] as well as worked on the James River and Kanawha Canal. Upon moving to Waynesboro, Gallaher purchased a piece of land near the Virginia Central Railroad and built a home, Rose Hall, a substantial brick house that became a center of gatherings, weddings and balls before, during and after the war. Hugh Gallaher moved his family into the home once it was completed in 1848.

By the mid-1850s, Hugh Gallaher had three daughters and four sons and had accumulated significant wealth and land in and around Waynesboro. The clan became one of the most prominent families in the area.[17] One of Gallaher's daughters, Miss Sallie Bowen Gallaher, married Captain Hugh McGuire of the 11th Virginia Regiment Cavalry, Company E. Captain McGuire was the brother of Stonewall Jackson's famous

Top: Lieutenant William Bowen Gallaher of Company E, 1st Virginia Cavalry Regiment, in uniform, with Virginia state seal belt plate, revolver and cavalry sword. *Courtesy Library of Congress.*

Right: DeWitt Clinton Gallaher was originally assigned as a captain and aide-de-camp to General John D. Imboden's staff. Gallaher also served in Company E in the 1st Virginia Cavalry as a courier for General J.E.B. Stuart. He later served under General Fitzhugh Lee and General Thomas L. Rosser. *Courtesy University of Virginia Library.*

Frances Amelia Briscoe married William Bowen Gallaher Sr. on August 8, 1864, near Charlestown, Virginia (now West Virginia). In December 1864, Mrs. Gallaher attempted to reach her husband's home in Waynesboro. She got as far as Winchester, where she was taken prisoner by General Phil Sheridan. This image shows Mrs. Gallaher being held prisoner at Sheridan's headquarters. After being held for a week, a Judge Baker and a Mrs. Baker (cousins) came to headquarters and claimed that she was their employee and the governess for their children. She was subsequently released into their custody. She continued on to Waynesboro shortly thereafter. *Courtesy Waynesboro Public Library.*

physician, Dr. Hunter McGuire. The couple was married at Rose Hall on January 12, 1865. Those in attendance included Major General Fitzhugh Lee (nephew of General Robert E. Lee) and Henry Kyd Douglas, who authored *I Rode with Stonewall.* Also present was Reverend W.T. Richardson, the same Presbyterian preacher who had given the benediction when the Valley Rangers marched off to Harper's Ferry in April 1861.[18] The wedding took place at eight o'clock in the evening, and the dancing and socializing lasted until the wee hours of the morning.

Just eleven months later, Mrs. McGuire would give birth to a daughter on November 8. But Captain McGuire would never see his daughter. He was mortally wounded at Amelia Springs, just four days before Lee surrendered. Brother-in-law DeWitt Gallaher would later write of him, "Hugh McGuire was captain of Co. E [51st Virginia Infantry]. He married my sister, Sallie, January 12th, 1865 and [was] killed on Lee's retreat, dying at Amelia Springs, Virginia. No braver trooper ever lived!"[19]

Hugh Gallaher would eventually come to own farms, a mill and a tannery. His wartime activities are somewhat mysterious and were a matter of controversy, even after his death in 1886. Local Waynesboro historian

The parlor at Rose Hall. *Courtesy Waynesboro Public Library.*

George Hawke authored an unpublished manuscript in 1988 titled "Hugh Gallaher: Yankee or Rebel?" Through his research, Hawke revealed that Gallaher petitioned the Southern Claims Commission[20] on April 15, 1871, for "property belonging to your petitioner which was during said Civil War, taken and carried away by the United States troops and applied to the use and benefit of the United States Army."[21] This commission allowed Southerners who had remained loyal to the Union during the war to file for reimbursement from the federal government for property losses they had suffered. Gallaher's attorneys claimed that the value of the property taken from their client was $32,587.50.

In Gallaher's petition, he claimed that the property was taken beginning in June 1864 by soldiers in General David Hunter's army after the Battle of Piedmont, then by soldiers under the command of Major General Alfred T.A. Torbert in September 1864 and, finally, by Union general Phil Sheridan's army during the Battle of Waynesboro. The petition further noted that "no vouchers or receipts were given for any of this property." These claims, along with the required testimony of witnesses, often provided a detailed and unique glimpse into the wartime lives of Southerners. Such was the case with Hugh Gallaher.

Gallaher had a number of prominent citizens testify on his behalf, including Stonewall Jackson's former quartermaster, Major John A. Harman;

local judge John Harris; and Virginia senator John F. Lewis. A sampling of the property listed in Gallaher's claim includes the following:

25 Head of fat cattle
15000 pounds of tobacco
80 barrels of flour
200 bushels of wheat
15 large Hogs
1100 Bushels of Corn
1250 Pounds of Bacon
1 Barrel of Molasses
1 Sorrel Horse[22]

Most of the testimony given by witnesses who supported Gallaher's claim corroborated the value and quantity of items listed by him. Hawke noted that John Harman "proved to be an articulate and slippery witness. At times he fenced with the Commissioners, and successfully defended his contention that Hugh Gallaher was loyal to the Union."[23]

But while the inventory may well have been accurate, Gallaher's claim that he met

Top: Hugh Lafferty Gallaher. *Courtesy Waynesboro Public Library.*

Left: Hugh Gallaher and his four sons, 1871. *Courtesy Waynesboro Public Library.*

30

the requirement of remaining loyal to the Union during the war was, at best, suspect. In addition to having two sons who served in the Confederate army, Mrs. Gallaher, along with the Gallaher daughters, was known for making "virulent anti-Union statements."[24]

The older of the Gallaher boys, William, was twenty-one when he enlisted on May 2, 1861. Little brother DeWitt was not yet sixteen in the spring of 1861 and, at the time, a student at Washington College in Lexington, forty miles south of Waynesboro. DeWitt would follow in his brother's footsteps and join the Confederate army in 1863. Both boys had attended the Waynesboro Academy[25] in their youth. William was at Virginia Military Institute for one year before enlisting. DeWitt first served as aide-de-camp to General John D. Imboden in 1863. Imboden was from neighboring Staunton. The younger Gallaher noted the following in the introduction to his personal diary notes after the war:

> *I accepted a position on General John D. Imboden's staff with the rank of Captain, as aide-de-camp, while his command was operating in the Shenandoah Valley. Though he was very kind to me and I was "messed" with him and his staff and we had orderlies and colored servants and everything to make a soldier's life comparatively pleasant, I very foolishly (I now think) became afraid the war would end without my being in some big battle. So I, in October, 1863, resigned all the comforts of a staff officer and joined as a private in Co E, 1st Virginia Cavalry, then down with General R.E. Lee's army on the Rapidan River, Culpepper County, Virginia.[26]*

DeWitt Gallaher returned to his hometown during the Battle of Waynesboro and came close to being taken prisoner, but he did not participate directly in the fighting. After arriving in Harper's Ferry in April 1861, brother William wrote the following letter to his "Dear Pa":

> *I wrote to Ma from the Ferry on Saturday & I will now write you a few lines. We got here yesterday from the Ferry, & am quartered in a large hall opposite the United States Hotel & am boarding at the Central & Union Hotels. We have a very good time but I dont know how long it will last. I send you by James Patrick a Minnie Musket a present to you from John Lipscomb. I will get the moulds when I go to the Ferry. We dont know how long we will stay here. Tell Ma I stopped in Shepherdstown yesterday & got my dinner at Grandma's. I saw all the folks they are all well. Grandpa came up here with me & got his supper at Mr Rawlins. I went over this*

morning to see Mr Rawlins & family. They are all well & very glad to see me. Mrs R sent her son up for me. They send their love to all of you. Mollie says Sallie must write to her. They say Clinton & Sallie must come down this summer. I am very well satisfied with camp life & think I can get along very well. Grandpa says you & Ma must come to see them this summer. I was introduced to Maj Robinson this morning he sends his respects to you. He seemed glad to hear you were improving. He invited me to his house for dinner. I intend going to Mr Rawlins tomorrow again. I want to see his tan yard. Our men behave very well. Any letters you write direct to Harpers Ferry care Capt James Patrick. There is a great many union men here & black Republicans but I think we can get along with them without any difficulty. My [horse] stands it very well. I attend to her myself. I could have gotten Alfred Plumb to attend to her for $5 per week but I concluded I had better save it as all the boys attend to theirs. Tell Ma I will take good care of myself & not keep any bad company. How are you getting along tanning. I saw Mr Kiblinger as I came up & also Mr Connoly in Shepherdstown. I will go down and stay half day or so at Shepherdstown if we stay here. Capt Patrick says he will write to you in a short time. The Pistol you sent him he did not need he was made a present of one when we got here. He loaned it to James McClung who is a member of our company he will take good care of it. Should you need it let me know & I will send it to you if I have a chance. As I have written an unusually long letter & have some business to attend to I will stop. Write soon give my love to all. I will write again in a few days. Tell them all to write me.

Your Son
W B Gallaher[27]

In William's next letter, addressed to "Ma" and dated May 15, 1861, he advised his mother to tell his Pa to "keep a sharp look out in the farm yard & at the stable"—evidently worried about thieves or marauding Union soldiers. In the letter that follows this one, William shared a story about an accident in camp involving fellow Waynesboro resident Elliot Fishburne. In reading his account, one wonders if he was making an attempt at some deadpan humor over what could have been a mortal wounding:

I am writing this letter in the Hospital. The house belonging to the states occupied by Ball Superintendent who has left. It is a beautiful place. I and John Lipscomb are staying here with Elliott Fishburne. He was shot in Martinsburg the day before yesterday by the accidental discharge of a pistol in one of the boys hands. It was one of the old revolvers or it would have killed him. He was sitting at a table when one of the boys came up & was snapping the pistol in 2 feet of his face & it went off. The ball entered his left cheek knocked out two of his teeth & fractured his jawbone & struck his tongue. They dont know where the ball is. I think he swallowed it. [28]

In reading soldiers' diaries and letters from the Civil War, one often sees references to God and the Christian faith. Stories of camp church services and prayer meetings are frequently recounted. Christianity was much more central to nineteenth-century Americans' daily lives than it is to us today, particularly to those who were so close to death on a daily basis. Family members back home often sent reminders that they were praying for their soldier boys and would encourage them to seek God's protection and to remember their religious upbringing. One of William's letters, undated and addressed to his mother, reveals that he was aware of his family's concern over his spiritual well-being and offers some reassurance that he was not neglecting his faith:

I read the tract you sent me & will read a portion of my Bible & the book Sallie put in my trunk everyday. I am very well & am as well satisfied as I could be under the circumstances. Of course I would like to be with you all & hope if spared by Providence to be at some future day I may get up in August to see you all. [29]

William continued in the same letter, perhaps sensing his mother's concern over what vices he might be exposed to in camp life, and related Elliott Fishburne's apparent progress since swallowing that pistol ball. He closed with assurances to his mother that he is faring well:

We have the best behaved boys in the camps in our tent. Elliott is looking as well as ever…We live very well. When we get in the country we go to the farm houses & get as much as we can eat. Some of the boys had strawberries given them by the country people. I will get some the next time I go out if I can. Ma you must excuse bad writing my paper is not ruled very well. I will write often to you. Write soon. Give my love to all kiss the little folks for me. Give my respect to all. God Bless you all. [30]

William was soon exposed to the battle of First Manassas and wrote to his father, describing some of the carnage he witnessed:

Manassas Junction July 22nd, 1861

Dear Father,

We had a Large Battle here yesterday, about 40 miles from here. It lasted near 11 hours. Our loss is estimated at 5000 killed & wounded. We had some taken prisoners. The enemy loss is put at 18,000. I don't know how true these estimates are. We have taken at least 600 prisoners & 36 pieces of artillery...I was out on the Battle Field with Gen's Beauregard & Johnson. The cannon balls and shell fell very close to me, but through Providence I was not hurt. Gen B had his horse killed under him. Gen. Jackson's Brigade suffered very much. Two of the West Augusta Guard were killed and Wm Barkins of the Augusta Rifles was killed. Both companies had a few wounded...After the battle I rode over the field. I never saw such a horrible sight in my life. The ground was covered with dead Yankees and we had a great many killed and wounded.[31]

A few weeks later, William Gallaher penned a letter from Fairfax Courthouse to his mother, notifying her of a promotion and expressing his aggravation at gluttonous Yankee soldiers and a desire to resign from the army, which he did due to health reasons:

I wrote Pa a few lines yesterday but thought he might not get it. I am tolerably well. We are encamped at this place which is something larger than Fishersville. It is a rather poor looking town. The Yankees had been here some time & ate pretty near everything that they could find... Well I have rec'd a commission at last as a 2nd Lieut so whenever I get tired of soldiering I can resign & come home which I think I shall do in a few weeks.[32]

Going back to the elder Gallaher's Southern Claims Commission claim, one of the witnesses against the validity of Gallaher's claim was a federal revenue service agent by the name of William H. Frenger, who addressed the following letter to Dr. O.F. Presbry, a supervisor for the Internal Revenue Service:

Greenville, VA
April 21, 1871

My Dear Sir

I see by the Washington Chronicle of 19th, instant that Hugh L. Gallaher, of Waynesboro, Augusta County, Virginia, is claiming reimbursement for cattle, forage and farm produce taken by Union Army during the rebellion.

I would like to know if his loyalty during those trying days entitles him to the rare favor he seeks.

I am creditably advised that Mr. G was an earnest advocate of the vile heresy of secession; that he was appointed an agent and accepted a mission to Europe for the rebel cause and against the government he now desires to pay him. I consider this consistency: doing what he could then to destroy our government, and now wishing to bear off a part of her treasure.

I have written this much in order to protect the government from being wronged and to raise my own voice against paying men for property who aided to defeat our cause; and I have addressed this to you, feeling that you had at heart the good of our country, and would sound the alarm, and have the facts looked into before Mr. G or anybody else is paid.

Very Respectfully,
William H. Frenger[33]

In addition to the fact that both DeWitt and William Gallaher served in the Confederate army, as well as the knowledge that the Gallaher women were known to hold rather unsympathetic opinions of Yankees, Hugh Gallaher's activities during the war—both alleged and known—cast even further doubt on his claim that he did not support the Confederate cause, as he stated in his original claim that "your petitioner was loyal to the cause and the Government of the United States during the war, and was so loyal before and at the time of the taking of the property for which claim is made."[34]

Beyond the original petition, filed by his attorneys, Gallaher also signed a sworn oath that included the additional claim that he "did not voluntarily serve in the Confederate army or navy either as an officer or soldier or sailor or an any other capacity at any time during the late rebellion, that he never voluntarily furnished any stores, supplies or other material aid to the said Confederate army or navy or to the Confederate Government or to any offices, department or adherent of the same in support thereof, and that he never voluntarily accepted or exercised the functions of any office whatsoever under, or yielded support to the said Confederate Government."[35]

Frenger's accusation that Gallaher was an "agent" of the Confederate government was supported by Enos Richmond, who served as a special agent for the commission. Richmond's accusations against Gallaher were even more serious and detailed than Frenger's had been. In a letter to the commission dated April 22, 1871, Richmond claimed that Gallaher was actually involved in blockade running for the Confederacy:

Dear Sir:

I promised to write you when I reached home, but have been so busy since my return that I found no time until now to keep my promise. I have just seen a paragraph in the Washington Chronicle *saying that the claim of Hugh L. Gallaher of Waynesboro, Virginia, had been heard by your board. The claim is for over thirty-two thousand dollars. Mr. Gallaher may be a Loyal man now. He is a native of Pennsylvania, but has resided in Virginia about thirty years. In 1862 he was engaged in blockade running, went to England and shipped to Richmond a large quantity of medicines for the Confederate States. I am also informed, on what I consider good authority, that he was an especial agent of the Confederate States at that time.*[36]

Richmond's letter goes on to recount other falsified claims by other southerners and asserts that he personally knew "nearly every loyal man for many miles and the number is very small indeed that have just claims against the Government." Obviously, Richmond did not count Gallaher among that number. The notion that Gallaher was a blockade runner was supported, at least circumstantially, by some of Gallaher's own sworn testimony. On January 24, 1873, Gallaher, along with a number of other witnesses, gave testimony to the commissioner of claims. Gallaher's testimony included the following exchange:

Question: In what year did you go to Europe?
Answer: I sailed from Wilmington on the 26ᵗʰ of August, 1862, and landed in Southampton in October 1862. I took my second son to Wilmington and to Charleston. I tried to get a passage for him at both places, but was unable to do so. My intention was to put him to school at Rugby in England, and let him remain there during the war. Besides, I had been speculating in various things. I bought all the tobacco I could get with Confederate

money, and sold that, and converted that, and everything else I could get into sterling. I took that sterling to Europe.

Question: Where did you sail from?
Answer: From Wilmington, North Carolina.

Question: In what ship?
Answer: The steamer Kate.

Question: Blockade runner?
Answer: Yes sir.

Question: What Captain?
Answer: Captain Lockwood. We went on board of her to Nassau, and then went from there to St. Thomas.[37]

The *Kate* (later christened the USS *Malvern*) was an English-built vessel and was under the command of Captain Thomas J. Lockwood. Lockwood was particularly well known—and hated—by the United States government. Lockwood's reputation within the Union army and government was well earned. He was regarded as somewhat of a legend among blockade runners.

Malvern Kate at the Norfolk Navy Yard, Virginia, circa 1865, while serving as flagship of the North Atlantic Blockading Squadron, per *U.S. Naval Historical Center Photograph*. Note the ruined buildings in the background. *Text and image Library of Congress.*

Lockwood was never captured and made a number of successful blockade runs while commanding the *Kate*. William Morrison Robinson Jr. described Lockwood's reputation and the *Kate* in his book *The Confederate Privateers*:

> *He made of this vessel one of the most renowned packet steamers of the beleaguered Confederacy. It is said she made more than forty successful voyages into Dixieland before being wrecked, near the entrance of the Cape Fear River during the late fall of 1862. So great a thorn in the side of the blockaders did the Kate become that twice boat expeditions, under cover of night, were sent in to try to cut her out at her Wilmington anchorage… The favorite cargo of Captain Lockwood was munitions of war; and, on occasion when asked what he had carried on his last voyage, he humorously replied, "Food for the North."*[38]

Just prior to the outbreak of the war, Lockwood captained a steam packet that was hired to escort members of the military and citizens of Charleston, South Carolina, on a tour of Charleston Harbor. Aboard the *Caroline* were Pierre Gustave Toutant Beauregard and States Rights Gist. A smaller ship, with a band on board, accompanied the *Caroline* and followed close behind. While conducting the tour, Lockwood ordered his ship to sail close to Fort Sumter so that the Yankees garrisoned there could enjoy a rousing rendition of "Dixie" played by the band on the smaller ship. Lockwood's daring and successes would earn him the sobriquet "Father of the Trade."

The mere possibility that Gallaher was in any way connected to Lockwood and the *Kate* was by itself likely enough to cast a pall over any hopes he had of having his claim approved, even though Gallaher claimed that his presence on the *Kate* was strictly personal, rather than government business.

Of course, there was much more testimony and letters, both pro and con, regarding Hugh Gallaher's claim. Finally, on December 8, 1873, the commission rendered its decision. Despite the testimony against Gallaher and his presence on the *Kate*, the commission's wording in the unsigned decision was apparently a close call. One passage in the decision indicates that the commissioners struggled with their final verdict:

> *The testimony in this case was taken by the commissioners personally. The claimant was a resident of Waynesboro, Augusta Co., Va., a man of wealth and considerable prominence in the community. In addition to farming, he owned and carried on a tanyard. His appearance and deportment as a witness were in the highest degree favorable, and after his positive claim to*

sympathy with the Union cause throughout the war, we are slow to come to the conclusion that such statement is not entitled to unqualified credit.[39]

After several more paragraphs explaining their reasoning, the commissioners came to the following conclusion, making special note of Gallaher's association with the *Kate*:

That he was regarded by the Confederate authorities as loyal, he could point to the fact that he was permitted to go and return from Richmond ad libitum. In 1862 he went to Richmond, thence to Wilmington, N.C., ran the blockade in a vessel bound to Nassau, thence to England…purchased medical supplies for the Confederate government which were smuggled into and sold to the Confederacy, the claimant sharing in the profits.

We cannot adjudge Mr. Gallaher loyal within the meaning of the statute, the claim is therefore disallowed.[40]

Even though that ended Hugh Gallaher's claim as far as the United States government was concerned, the investigation into his wartime activities continued. George Hawke noted that this was due to the fact that the clerks researching records in connection with Gallaher's case never received "any order to stop." The results of their research were meticulously catalogued and filed. Of all the additional information discovered after the commission's denial of Gallaher's claim, the most interesting, as well as damning, was discovered on page 268 of Letter Book No. 2, Engineering Bureau, War Department, CSA: "Endorsement on letter from Mr. H.L. Gallaher, dated Richmond, Jan 26, 1863, claiming damages for injuries done to his boat Catherine by [CSA] tug.—Engineering Bureau, February 5th, 1863."[41]

The same information is noted in the U.S. War Department's archives, Book 2, page 413, dated June 30, 1873. Evidently, Gallaher was, in fact, a blockade runner and privateer for the Confederacy and committed perjury during his claim hearing. Given the fact that he should have known that this information would likely be discovered at some point, it is somewhat surprising that a man of his stature and position would risk prison and further financial ruin in making false and misleading statements to the commissioners.

The *Catherine* (more accurately, the *Catherine T. Dix*) is mentioned in various sources and was involved in an incident on April 11, 1862. Apparently, this is the incident that caused the damage referred to by the Engineering Bureau (CSA) file dated February 5, 1863. On April 11, 1862, the CSS *Virginia* (*Merrimack*) and the CSS *Jamestown*, along with five other Confederate vessels, left Norfolk and set sail for Hampton Roads with the intention of luring the Union blockade ships into a battle. The Yankees declined the offer, allowing the Rebels to sail into the harbor and "capture" three merchant ships. Two were brigs, and one was Gallaher's schooner, the *Catherine T. Dix*.

William Robinson described the incident:

> *Nevertheless, the* Virginia *remained mistress of Hampton Roads, and, though offering combat without reserve, could never entice the ironclad* Monitor, *the ram* Vanderbilt, *or any of the enemy's fleet into engagement. On one occasion when the* Virginia *offered battle, and was refused, Commodore Tattnall sent the little wooden gunboats* Thomas Jefferson *and* Raleigh *within the enemy's lines to cut out three transports. The enemy suffered the two Confederate steamers to capture and tow away the brigs* Marcus *and* Saboah *and the schooner* Catherine T. Dix, *without responding to the taunt.*[42]

Part of the "taunt" included having the merchant ships lower and then hoist their flags "Union-side down." It was during the tow back to Norfolk that Gallaher's ship, the *Catherine T. Dix*, was damaged and for which he would subsequently request compensation from the Confederate government. Gallaher's great-grandson, William B. Gallaher, related the following to George Hawke regarding his ancestor's Civil War activities:

> *He* [Hugh] *and Col. Ben Ficklin, an agent for the Confederacy, ran the blockade from Wilmington, N.C. in 1863, to Nassau and then on to England to purchase supplies in Europe for the C.S.A. It is my understanding that they made several trips to England and France to procure supplied needed by the C.S.A. during the war. I understand his sailing vessel was the* Catherine.[43]

After Hugh Gallaher died in 1886, son DeWitt (who was by then an attorney), along with some other heirs, lobbied Virginian congressman Henry St. George Tucker III to introduce legislation that would have overridden the commission's prior denial of Gallaher's claim. On June 6, 1894, Congressman Tucker introduced *H.R. 7371: A Bill for the Relief of the Estate of Hugh L. Gallaher Authorizing Payment to Estate in Amount of $32,587.50.* The bill was never brought to the floor for a vote.

Hugh Gallaher was a man of contradictions, nuances and mixed loyalties. Ironically, the very day of the Battle of Waynesboro, the Gallaher household entertained Confederate general Jubal Early at breakfast and Union general Philip Sheridan at supper. And George Hawked noted that "[f]amily lore states that when Sheridan learned that Hugh Gallaher was a Masonic Knight Templar, he posted a guard at the home to prevent vandalism."[44]

But more than anything else, Gallaher seemed to be a pragmatist:

> *Hugh Gallaher had many admirable traits, and these should not be obscured by his questionable claim for reimbursement, or the possibility that he was a double-agent…an evenhanded view of the claims file shows both good and bad: friends portrayed him as a kind and honest man, and he was; ardent Unionists portray him as an opportunistic and calculating man, and he was (what businessman isn't?); his family and ex-slaves portray him as a gentlemanly and sympathetic man, and he was that too.*[45]

Gallaher's loyalties seemed to be more economic and practical than they were ideological or political, and they were representative of many others who lived in the shadow of the Blue Ridge during those turbulent years.

Chapter 2

EARLY SHIVERS AND STARVES

The end of the year and cold as blazes.
—Confederate soldier W.H. Alexander, December 31, 1864

The man who would command the Confederate forces at the Battle of Waynesboro, Jubal Anderson Early, was born on November 16, 1816, in Franklin County, Virginia. In his autobiography, he provided this brief sketch of his life up to the time he graduated from West Point:

> *According to the record in the family Bible, I was born on the third day of November, 1816, in the County of Franklin, in the State of Virginia. My father, Joab Early, who is still living, is a native of the same county, and while resident there, he enjoyed the esteem of his fellow-citizens and held several prominent public positions, but in the year 1847, he removed to the Kanawha Valley in Western Virginia. My mother's maiden name was Ruth Hairston, and she was likewise a native of the County of Franklin, her family being among the most respected citizens. She died in the year 1832, leaving ten children surviving her, I being the third child and second son. She was a most estimable lady, and her death was not only the source of the deepest grief to her immediate family, but caused universal regret in the whole circle of her acquaintances.*
>
> *Until I was sixteen I enjoyed the benefit of the best schools in my region of country and received the usual instruction in the dead languages and elementary mathematics. In the spring of 1833, while General Jackson was President,*

General Jubal Early. *Courtesy Library of Congress.*

I received, through the agency of our member of Congress, the Hon. N.H. Claiborne, an appointment as cadet in the United States Military Academy at West Point.

I repaired to the Academy at the end of May and was admitted about the first of June in the same year. I went through the usual course and graduated in the usual time, in June, 1837. There was nothing worthy of particular note in my career at West Point. I was never a very good student, and was sometimes quite remiss, but I managed to attain a respectable stand in all my studies. My highest stand in any branch was in military and civil engineering and that was sixth. In the general standing on graduation my position was eighteenth in a class of fifty.

I was not a very exemplary soldier and went through the Academy without receiving any appointment as a commissioned or non-commissioned officer in the corps of cadets. I had very little taste for scrubbing brass, and cared very little for the advancement to be obtained by the exercise of that most useful art.

Among those graduating in my class were General Braxton Bragg, Lieutenant General John C. Pemberton, Major Generals Arnold Elzey and Wm. H.T. Walker, and a few others of the Confederate Army; and Major Generals John Sedgwick, Joseph Hooker, and Wm. H. French and several Brigadier Generals of minor note in the Federal Army. Among my contemporaries at West Point were General Beauregard, Lieutenant General Ewell, Major General Edward Johnson and some others of distinction in the Confederate Army; Major Generals McDowell and Meade and several others in the Federal Army.

The whole of my class received appointments in the United States Army shortly after graduation.[46]

After being appointed a second lieutenant, Early was ordered to Fort Monroe, Virginia, in August 1837. From there, he sailed to Florida in October of the same year. The Second Seminole War was still being fought, and Early related his first battle experience with the Florida Indians:

I went through the campaign of 1837–8 under General Jessup, from the St. John's River south into the Everglades, and was present at a skirmish with the Indians on the Lockee Hatchee, near Jupiter Inlet, in January, 1838. This was my first "battle," and though I heard some bullets whistling among the trees, none came near me, and I did not see an Indian.[47]

But since Early noted that "[it] had not been my purpose to remain permanently in the army,"[48] he resigned, returned to his native Franklin County and began studying law in the fall of 1838. He was licensed to practice law in 1840, and in the spring of 1841, he was elected to represent Franklin County in the Virginia legislature. At just twenty-four years of age, Jubal Early became the youngest member of the oldest legislative body in the western hemisphere. Defeated in the next election cycle, Early then received an appointment as the Commonwealth's attorney for the circuit court in Franklin and neighboring Floyd County. It now appeared that Early was destined to live out his life as a country lawyer and politician in rural Virginia. But war would intervene to alter Early's career path. First there was the Mexican-American War. Appointed as a major with a Virginia regiment of volunteers, Early was mustered back into the United States Army on January 7, 1847. Early would serve in garrison duties and, for a brief time, as governor of Monterey, Mexico. Some of Early's personality is revealed in his autobiography when he wrote of his time as governor of Monterey:

It was generally conceded by officers of the army and Mexicans that better order reigned in the city during the time I commanded there, than had ever before existed, and the good conduct of my men won for them universal praise.[49]

When the war was over, Early returned to Virginia and resumed his legal career. Jubal Early stood about six feet tall and weighed close to 170 pounds. He walked with a stoop due to rheumatoid arthritis—a condition that first afflicted him in Mexico. Early constantly chewed tobacco and, when excited, would shift his quid from one cheek to the other. Author and fellow Confederate soldier John S. Wise noted the following about Early's appearance and persona:

He was eccentric in many ways,—eccentric in appearance, in voice, in manner of speech. Although he was not an old man, his shoulders were so stooped and rounded that he brought his countenance to a vertical position with difficulty. He wore a long, thin, straggling beard. His eyes were very small, dark, deep-set, and glittering, and his nose aquiline. His step was slow, shuffling, and almost irresolute. I never saw a man who looked less like a soldier. His voice was a piping treble, and he talked with a long-drawn whine or drawl. His opinions were expressed unreservedly, and he was most emphatic and denunciatory, and startlingly profane.

His likes and dislikes he announced without hesitation, and, as he was filled with strong and bitter opinions, his conversation was always racy and pungent. His views were not always correct, or just, or broad; but his wit was quick, his satire biting, his expressions were vigorous, and he was interestingly lurid and picturesque.[50]

Early's reputation for profanity is well known—so much so that Robert E. Lee would refer to Early as his "old bad man." Lee's moniker was more jousting than disapproving, and Early held Lee in high regard. John Wise gave a hint of that admiration with this observation:

General Early, in my opinion, said things about his superiors, the Confederate leaders, civic and military, and their conduct of affairs, sufficient to have convicted him a hundred times over before any court-martial. But his criticisms never extended to General Robert E. Lee. For Lee he seemed to have a regard and esteem and high opinion felt by him for no one else. Although General Lee had but recently been called to the command of the army, he predicted his great future with unerring judgment.[51]

Early attempted to explain his brusque manner in this way:

I was never blessed with popular or captivating manners, and the consequence was that I was often misjudged and thought to be haughty and disdainful in my temperament.[52]

His reputation for possessing a "haughty and disdainful" temperament could not be blamed solely on misjudgment, however. During the Civil War, he once ordered a regiment to the front line for what he perceived as dereliction of duty, "where he hoped every one of them would get killed and burn through all eternity."[53]

Jubal Early was initially a strong and vocal opponent of secession, as he explained in his autobiography:

> *When the question of practical secession from the United States arose, as a citizen of the State of Virginia, and a member of the Convention called by the authority of the Legislature of that State, I opposed secession with all the ability I possessed, with the hope that the horrors of civil war might be averted and that a returning sense of justice on the part of the masses of the Northern States would induce them to respect the rights of the people of the South.*
>
> *While some Northern politicians and editors were openly and sedulously justifying and encouraging secession, I was laboring honestly and earnestly to preserve the Union. As a member of the Virginia Convention, I voted against the ordinance of secession on its passage by that body, with the hope that even then, the collision of arms might be avoided and some satisfactory adjustment arrived at.*[54]

After Virginia voted to secede, Early claims to have wept "bitter tears of grief." Nonetheless, he could not turn his back on his native sod:

> *I at once recognized my duty to abide the decision of my native State, and to defend her soil against invasion. Any scruples which I may have entertained as to the right of secession were soon dispelled by the unconstitutional measures of the authorities at Washington and the frenzied clamor of the people of the North for war upon their former brethren of the South. I recognized the right of resistance and revolution as exercised by our fathers in 1776 and without cavil as to the name by which it was called, I entered the military service of my State, willingly, cheerfully, and zealously.*
>
> *When the State of Virginia became one of the Confederate States and her troops were turned over to the Confederate Government, I embraced the cause of the whole Confederacy with equal ardor, and continued in the service, with the determination to devote all the energy and talent I possessed to the common defence [sic]. I fought through the entire war, without once regretting the course I pursued, with an abiding faith in the justice of our cause.*[55]

Early's "energy and talent" would manifest itself early in the Civil War. First appointed as a general in the Virginia state militia, he then became a colonel in the Confederate army and the first commander of the 24th Virginia Infantry. In the later afternoon at the battle of First Manassas, on

July 21 1861, Early distinguished himself by leading a key counterattack against the Federal army's right flank along Chinn Ridge. Following that performance, Early was promoted to brigadier general. The following fifth of May, Early was wounded at the Battle of Williamsburg while attacking a much superior force. He returned home to Franklin County, recovered and was back in action within two months. Through the time leading up to the Battle of Waynesboro, Early would fight in a number of major battles: Seven Days Battles, Second Manassas, Antietam, Fredericksburg, Chancellorsville, Gettysburg and Cold Harbor. On May 31, 1864, Early was promoted to the rank of lieutenant general for his actions at the Battle of the Wilderness. "Old Jube's" early record in the war was mostly successful, and his reputation as a tough commander was a solid one.

But by the winter of 1864–65, those earlier days of success and glory were fading fast in the mind of Jubal Early. He would describe that winter as "a severe one."[56] Early spoke of the weather, but his words described the state of his army as well. Although the Confederate forces had been at a disadvantage from the very beginning of the war in terms of resources, things had become much worse by the end of 1864, particularly in the Shenandoah Valley. The Valley had been laid waste by "the Burning," Union general Phil Sheridan's systematic destruction of homes, barns, mills, crops and

Custer's division retiring from Mount Jackson in the Shenandoah Valley, October 7, 1864, by Alfred R. Waud. *Courtesy Library of Congress.*

livestock. And although Early's army was the only organized resistance left in the Valley, it had been "reduced to a starving and demoralized skeleton of what it had been in the fall of 1864." Starving and demoralized is precisely what General Ulysses S. Grant had in mind when he told Sheridan that he wanted "the Shenandoah Valley to remain a barren waste."[57]

A constant concern for both Union and Confederate quartermasters was forage for horses and mules. On average, each animal required three pounds of grain per day to survive. The task of providing this became increasingly difficult toward the end of the war, particularly in the once bountiful "Breadbasket of the Confederacy."

The barren waste condition of the Valley during those winter months following the Burning was confirmed by soldiers on both sides, including Sergeant S.A. Dunning, who was attached to General Early's headquarters when he wrote on February 4, 1865, "I am positive forage is very scarce… The citizens in the Valley are very destitute."[58]

A private serving with the 18th Virginia Cavalry, Norval Baker, gave the following account regarding forage conditions in the Valley during the winter of 1864–65:

> My horse looked more like a fence rail with legs than a horse. All the feed in the Valley from Staunton North had been burnt by Sheridan's army and the [Confederate] cavalry in the Valley had to break up in small bunches and go into the little valleys and mountain coves in West Virginia to get feed for their horses.[59]

Things were so bad and morale among Confederate soldiers was so low during this time that local historian Curtis Bowman noted it when he wrote of an anonymous letter that several of Early's men (who were at the time in winter camp at Fishersville) wrote to Confederate president Jefferson Davis "asking that efforts to negotiate a viable peace be stepped up." Rationalizing that "the South was losing the war, their families were suffering as much as they, and it was futile to continue in a 'no-win' situation." According to Bowman, Davis added some of his own "caustic remarks" and forwarded the letter to General Lee, who then sent it back to Early. Bowman wrote that the letter was "found in Early's supply wagon, captured by Gen. Custer on Main Street [Waynesboro] Hill."[60]

General Sheridan noted in a letter to Major General George Crook the following day that there was "[g]reat suffering for want of forage."[61] Historian and native Shenandoah Valley resident John Heatwole summed up the consequences and successful objective of Sheridan's actions and how they would affect Early's army this way: "The burning of the Valley…created conditions that could no longer support a mobile Confederate force in numbers that would be of more than a passing concern to the Union high command."[62]

In addition to Sheridan's burning of the Valley, the drought the previous summer had made matters even worse. Early mentioned some of the extreme measures to which he had to resort to hold his fragile army together during the months leading up to the Battle of Waynesboro:

> *The great drought during the summer of 1864 had made the corn crop in the Valley a very short one, and, as Sheridan had destroyed a considerable quantity of small grain and hay, I found it impossible to sustain the horses of my cavalry and artillery where they were, and forage could not be obtained from elsewhere. I was therefore compelled to send Fitz. Lee's two brigades to General Lee, and Lomax's cavalry was brought from across the Blue Ridge, where the country was exhausted of forage, and sent west into the counties of Pendleton, Highland, Bath, Alleghany and Greenbrier, where hay could be obtained. Rosser's brigade had to be temporarily disbanded, and the men allowed to go to their homes with their horses, to sustain them, with orders to report when called on—one or two companies, whose homes were down the Valley, being required to picket and scout in front of New Market.*[63]

By December 1864, General Robert E. Lee's circumstances in Petersburg had necessitated a decision that would further weaken Early's already disadvantaged army. Lee ordered three of Early's divisions (commanded by Major General John B. Gordon, Brigadier General Bryan Grimes and Brigadier General John Pegram, respectively) east to strengthen his lines. Lee's order left Early with the roughly 1,200 men of General Gabriel Wharton's Division. And by the time the Battle of Waynesboro would commence, that number would dwindle even further. This was a far cry from the 12,000 men Early commanded after his defeat at the hands of Union general Phil Sheridan at Cedar Creek in October 1864.

After much of Early's army boarded trains headed to Petersburg that cold December, what remained established winter camp in Fishersville (a small hamlet about six miles west of Waynesboro), beginning construction of their winter quarters on Christmas Day. Early made his personal headquarters in Staunton, roughly six miles farther west of Fishersville.

The stinging memory of Cedar Creek's defeat at the hands of Phil Sheridan likely filled Early's mind during those dreary days and nights in December 1864 as his hungry army shivered in camp at Fishersville and as his scouts and pickets kept a wary eye on the movements of his old adversary encamped at Winchester. Lee's "old bad man" knew that he had likely not seen the last of Phil Sheridan. Early's skeleton of an army would soon face Sheridan's superior forces at Waynesboro for the last battle of the Civil War in the Shenandoah Valley. Although Sheridan's nickname was "Little Phil," the Yankee general would loom large in Early's memory for the rest of his life.

Chapter 3

SHERIDAN BURNS AND BOASTS

It is an insult to civilization and to God to pretend the Laws of War justify such warfare.

—Henry Kyd Douglas

The future commander[64] of Union forces at the Battle of Waynesboro, Philip Henry Sheridan, was born on March 6, 1831, in New York.[65] He was perhaps best known by many contemporaries for his rapid rise through the Union ranks from an infantry division commander to lead the Cavalry Corps in the Army of the Potomac. His fame among Southerners would come from events less laudable.

As a boy growing up in Ohio, Sheridan worked as a clerk and bookkeeper in several dry goods stores but showed an early bent for the military. One boyhood incident recounted of Sheridan was perhaps indicative of his future as a cavalry general:

> *When about five years old, he was placed by some older boys, in fun, on the back of a spirited horse found grazing in the field near where he resided. The horse was started of [sic] at a run; but the animal getting frightened at something it had either seen or heard, or perhaps both, dashed along at break-neck pace over rails and fences, and without bit or bridle. Every one thought the child would have been killed; but to the surprise of all, the horse, after a run of many miles, arrived at the stable of a hotel, where it had with its owner been in the habit of stopping. Its sides were flecked with foam, and the animal was exhausted with fatigue—but the child was still on its back… The adventure*

Major General P.H. Sheridan, circa 1861–65. *Courtesy Library of Congress.*

became the subject of village wonder; and the room of the hotel, that evening, was the scene of a large assemblage of farmers, and others, who had gathered together to hear the story repeated; and to see the child who had ridden such an immense distance, without a saddle or bridle.[66]

An early biography noted Sheridan's interest in all things military:

Phil Sheridan was, from his earliest boyhood, a lover of soldiers. His eye danced and his heart beat whenever there was a drill of the village militia company. Every summer he would get a dozen of his school-mates, and persuade them that it was the best fun in the world to play soldier. His friend Cassell would let him have a sword of the sharpest and brightest tin, and, of course, Phil was always captain.[67]

This, along with another quality, would set Sheridan's course for life:

[B]esides his love of fun and soldiering, was that he never knew fear. He was always ready to stand his ground against any odds. The school-

master who taught him his earliest lessons has long since passed away; but his school-mates say that Phil Sheridan never studied in earnest until he thought he had a chance to go to West Point.[68]

Sheridan's record at West Point was anything but stellar, graduating thirty-fourth in a class of fifty-two in 1853. Even that rather unremarkable showing had been threatened by Sheridan's fierce temper. Historian and professor Paul Andrew Hutton told of the incident in September 1851 involving future Union general William R. Terrill[69] that almost cost Sheridan his career:

On the drill field late one afternoon cadet Sergeant William R. Terrill of Virginia ordered Sheridan to align himself properly in the ranks. There may have been more to it than that, perhaps some previous altercation. Terrill's imperious manner enraged Sheridan, and he lunged forward with his bayonet to strike his tormentor. For an instant, all the demons that hounded him for being Irish, Catholic, short, and ugly were loose, but he regained control before disaster and pulled back. A horrified Terrill reported the incident to his superiors, as duty required. Further enraged, Sheridan immediately sought out Terrill and attacked him, but this time with fists. At a wiry five-foot-six, Sheridan was no match for the larger Virginian and was saved from a sound thrashing by the intervention of an officer.[70]

Sheridan described the incident this way in his memoirs:

Terrill was a Cadet Sergeant, and, while my company was forming for parade, having given me an order, in what I considered an improper tone, to "dress" in a certain direction, when I believed I was accurately dressed, I fancied I had a grievance, and made toward him with a lowered bayonet, but my better judgment recalled me before actual contact could take place. Of course Terrill reported me for this, and my ire was so inflamed by his action that when we next met I attacked him, and a fisticuff engagement in front of barracks followed, which was stopped by an officer appearing on the scene. Each of us handed in an explanation, but mine was unsatisfactory to the authorities, for I had to admit that I was the assaulting party.[71]

Sheridan received a one-year suspension for his angry outburst. His attack against Terrill likely had as much to do with his disdain for southern culture as with any perceived personal affront from Terrill. Hutton noted that Sheridan "never fit into the aristocratic, southern clique that dominated social affairs at West Point. Rural, Irish Catholic and Whig, he felt ill at ease with the southerners, who prized refined manners and stately posturing."[72]

Sheridan always reckoned northerners superior to his southern counterparts, once telling a comrade years after the Civil War why he felt so. While riding past a schoolhouse, he remarked to his companion, "That is what made us superior to the South; the little white schoolhouse of the North gave us a great advantage. Education is invincible."[73] In later years, Sheridan would admit that his youthful anger regarding Terrill was "outrageous" and that he actually deserved much worse than a one-year suspension.[74]

Upon graduating West Point, Sheridan was assigned to the 1st U.S. Infantry at Fort Duncan, Texas, and was commissioned as a brevet second lieutenant. Sheridan then served at posts mostly in the Northwest, and by the time the Civil War broke out in 1861, he had risen to the rank of first lieutenant and was then quickly promoted to the rank of captain after Fort Sumter. In May 1862, Sheridan was made a colonel in the 2nd Michigan Cavalry. His leadership and bravery while leading that regiment in battle resulted in his being promoted to brigadier general in September 1862. Sheridan's reputation continued to grow, and his actions at Chattanooga garnered the admiration of General Ulysses S. Grant. His tenacity at the Battle of Missionary Ridge on November 25, 1863, would set Sheridan's ultimate—and infamous—destiny with the "Breadbasket of the Confederacy": the beautiful and bountiful Shenandoah Valley of Virginia. Grant took special note of Sheridan's performance at Missionary Ridge: "Sheridan showed his genius in that battle, and to him I owe the capture of most of the prisoners that were taken."[75]

In the spring of 1864, Grant, despite objections from General George Meade, offered Sheridan the command of the Army of the Potomac's cavalry. When Lee ordered Early down the Valley, the threat to Washington led Grant, in the summer of 1864, to give Sheridan command of the Army of the Shenandoah over the objections of President Lincoln—such was Grant's confidence in Sheridan. Thus, the set of circumstances that would lead to the eventual clash between Early and Sheridan on the banks of the South River at Waynesboro had been put into motion. Sheridan would first whip Early at Winchester (September 19, 1864), Fisher's Hill (September 21–22, 1864) and Tom's Brook (October 9, 1864) and then, in dramatic fashion, would ride into the Battle at Cedar Creek on October 19 and turn what would have been a Confederate victory by Early's army into yet another Union triumph.

General Phil Sheridan and his staff. *Left to right*: Major General Sheridan, Colonel Jos. Forsythe, Chief of Staff Merritt, Brigadier General Thomas C. Devins and Major General George A. Custer. *Courtesy Library of Congress.*

In addition to this string of victories, which demoralized Early's army, another campaign would be led by Sheridan that would also play a significant role in the last battle of the Shenandoah Valley—the previously mentioned thirteen-day suffering and tribulation for Valley citizens that would become known simply as "the Burning."

The Shenandoah Valley had, from the beginning of the war, posed a threat to the Union in more ways than one. First of all, it was *geographically* threatening. Its proximity to Washington made it a dangerous gateway to the Federal capital, and its terrain made it a virtual fortress. Hemmed in on both its eastern and western borders by major mountain ranges and split in the lower Valley by a smaller range, Confederate forces could use the terrain to outmaneuver and elude the Union army, as Stonewall Jackson had done during his legendary Valley Campaign of 1862.

Secondly, the Valley's "Breadbasket of the Confederacy" moniker was well deserved, as it was the primary supply source sustaining the Army of Northern Virginia, as well as other divisions of the Confederate army. Historian Kenneth E. Koons described the fertile Shenandoah:

During the first half of the nineteenth century, the Shenandoah Valley achieved wide renown as an immensely fertile and highly productive agricultural region. Valley farmers practiced mixed agriculture in which they produced a broad array of field crops—including corn, hay, and the various cereal grains—and kept on hand a full complement of the usual types of livestock such as horses, cattle, sheep, swine, and barnyard fowl. Although diversity of economic enterprise characterized Valley farming, wheat served as the crop of paramount importance…By the mid-nineteenth century, farmers of the Shenandoah Valley (defined here as comprising the counties of Frederick, Clarke, Shenandoah, Warren, Rockingham, Page, Augusta, Rockbridge, and Botetourt) worked only nine percent of the improved acres of farmland in Virginia but produced twenty-two percent of the Commonwealth's wheat crop. By this time, the Valley had emerged as one of the most productive wheat farming regions of the South. One historian's comparison of wheat productivity in ten multi-county regions of the South encompassing portions of Virginia, Tennessee, Kentucky, Missouri, and Georgia, shows that in 1850 farmers in a four-county portion of the Shenandoah Valley—the counties of Rockbridge, Augusta, Rockingham, and Page—produced almost twenty bushels of wheat per capita, while farmers of the other nine regions produced fewer than six bushels per capita.[76]

Given these facts, it comes as little surprise that Sheridan would convince Grant to allow him to focus on the Shenandoah Valley's bounty, and not just its military targets. Grant sent the following communication to Sheridan on August 26, 1864:

Give the enemy no rest, and if it is possible to follow the Virginia Central [rail] road, follow that far [to Charlottesville]. Do all the damage to railroads and crops you can. Carry off stock of all descriptions, and negroes, so as to prevent further planting. If the war is to last another year, we want the Shenandoah Valley to remain a barren waste.[77]

Grant had already indicated that he wanted Union troops to "eat out Virginia clear and clean as far as they go, so that crows flying over it for the balance of the season will have to carry their provender with them."[78] Sheridan would fulfill Grant's wishes with great efficiency in doing "all the damage"—even to those Valley citizens who were unsympathetic to the Confederate cause. Sheridan would later write in his memoirs that his village schoolmaster had applied the rod of discipline indiscriminately to misbehaving students: "[I]f unable to detect the real culprit when any offense had been committed, [he] would consistently apply the switch to the whole school without discrimination."[79] Valley residents might reasonably conclude that Sheridan carried with him the principle of punishing even the innocent in order to make absolutely certain that the guilty did not escape. Some recalling of incidents regarding Sheridan's burning of the Shenandoah Valley are important in understanding where both sides were—in terms of mindset and emotion—by the time the Battle of Waynesboro took place in March 1865. Although mentioned in numerous histories of the Civil War, historian John Heatwole noted that Sheridan's actions were "largely forgotten in the annals of military history because it involved intentionally taking the war to the civilian population."[80]

While military historians may have nearly forgotten the Burning, Valley residents did not.[81] Resentment would linger for generations, and with good cause. John Heatwole recounts one incident in his book *The Burning*:

> One group of tough, blue-clad horsemen descended on Reuben Swope's farm, which was on a side road about a half a mile north of town [Dayton]. Swope begged them to stop, but to no avail. His wife, Susanna, and their three grown daughters looked on in disbelief as the Northerners set all of the outbuildings on fire...One of the soldiers asked twenty-year-old Susan Swope, the youngest daughter, if she thought that the women of the Valley would ever forgive the Northern soldiers for burning their homes. A quick light flashed in her eyes as she replied, "Do you think if it were Southern soldiers burning the houses of your mothers and sisters they would be forgiven?"[82]

As they mounted to leave the Swope farm, the soldiers warned the family that if the fires burning the home were put out, they'd return and shoot them all dead. Nonetheless, as soon as the Federals were out of sight, the family began dousing the fires with water-filled slop buckets. But Reuben Swope became worried: "Fear for the lives of his wife and children prompted him to set the fires anew, thus becoming an unwilling yet compliant accomplice in the destruction of his own home."[83]

Such recollections and images would be hard for a family to forget. Not all Valley farmers were so cooperative. Heatwole recounted the story of one farmer who offered deadly resistance: Moses Fry. Fry owned a farm near the mouth of Crooked Run in Shenandoah County. Although generally considered to be a "good neighbor," Fry also had a reputation as being "big, mean and a brawler." He was not shy about defending his farm, his wife and his seven children. Fry's eldest son served in the 12th Virginia Cavalry under General Thomas L. Rosser. As raiders burned his barn, all Fry could do was seethe, knowing that he would endanger his family if he attempted anything foolish. But as soon as the Yankees left for the next farm, Fry and his family successfully put out the fire and saved the barn. Then Fry's wife called his attention to a single blue-clad horseman riding up the lane. Ascertaining what had just taken place, the Yankee soldier dismounted, drew his revolver and ordered the family to stand together. John Heatwole recounted what happened next:

> *The officer, keeping an eye on the family and especially Fry, gathered straw and other dry tinder in a pile beside a wall of the barn and ignited it. He relaxed a little as he watched the flames bite into the wall and stretch toward the roof. It was obvious he would not leave until he was sure the blaze was beyond control.*
>
> *... [Fry] turned away and walked slowly toward the house. The officer in his youth and inexperience must have assumed that the farmer had given up, because he made no effort to stop him. Fry closed the front door behind him, grabbed the rifle that stood beside it, and went upstairs. One of the front windows was slightly raised, and there he knelt, taking deadly aim at the young officer. The rifle cracked, and his target crumpled to the ground.*[84]

Fry descended the stairs and walked to the corpse. He then lifted and carried it to the now fully consumed barn, where he threw the lifeless body into the raging fire.

After the war, a number of biographers would defend Sheridan's burning of the Shenandoah Valley:

> *The rising generation, no doubt, may be interested in the early life and true character of the brainiest fighter and greatest battle tactician on either side of our great war. I find that many believe Sheridan was cruel, hard-hearted and loved war and its savagery, but I know he was kind and gentle of heart. On several occasions I sought to correct these wrong impressions, when the accusing party would point to his unnecessary devastation of the beautiful Shenandoah Valley, where Sheridan seemed to revel in destruction. The accuser was not aware that this was done in obedience to an order from General Grant, whom, I am sure, no one would accuse of cruelty. It was*

a wise and merciful order to destroy what an enemy subsisted upon, as it brought peace more speedily than the destruction of human life.[85]

Sheridan naturally offered his own justification for instituting total war:

You would suppose that the burning of the barns and mills and the taking of livestock and grain was the most horrible feature of the war; to hear the talk one would think so. General Grant's object, as well as mine, was to bring the war to a speedy close. We knew of no quicker or more merciful plan than to destroy the principal granary, the Shenandoah Valley. I am sure there is more mercy in destroying supplies than in killing their young men, which a continuance of the war would entail. If I had a barn full of wheat and a son, I would much sooner lose the barn and wheat than my son. That rich, productive valley was furnishing vast quantities of the wheat and other grain that was used by the Confederate army. The question was, must we destroy their supplies or kill their young men? We chose the former.[86]

Despite these defenses, some historians have judged the Yankee general and found him wanting. As historian John Heatwole quoted from Stephen Starr's three-volume work *Union Cavalry in the Civil War*:

The deliberate, planned devastation of the Shenandoah Valley has deservedly ranked as one of the grimmest episodes of a sufficiently grim war. Unlike the haphazard destruction caused by Sherman's bummers in Georgia, it was committed systematically, and by order.[87]

Many of Sheridan's own men—even those desensitized by the horrors of battle—could not help but be moved by this "grim episode." Union colonel James Harvey Kidd revealed the following in his memoirs after the war:

The mill in the little hamlet of Port Republic contained the means of livelihood—the food of the women and children whom the exigencies of war had bereft of their natural providers and, when they found that it was the intention to destroy that on which their very existence seemed to depend, their appeals to be permitted to have some of the flour before the mill was burned, were heartrending. What I saw there is burned into my memory. Women with children in their arms, stood in the street and gazed frantically upon the threatened ruin of their homes, while the tears rained down their cheeks. The anguish pictured in their faces would have melted any heart not seared by the horrors and "necessities" of war. It was too much for me and at the first moment that duty would permit, I hurried away from the scene.[88]

Some Union soldiers were even "willing to risk court-martial rather than continue to be agents in the destruction of civilian property." One member of the 1st New York Lincoln Cavalry later wrote that "[m]en who never flinched in the hottest fight declared they would have no hand in this burning."[89]

Confederates also took note of the terror and anguish brought on by the Burning. One of Early's staff officers, Henry Kyd Douglas, later wrote:

I try to restrain my bitterness at the recollection of the dreadful scenes I witnessed. I rode down the Valley with the advance after Sheridan's retreating cavalry beneath great columns of smoke which almost shut out the sun by day, and the red glare of bonfires, which, all across the Valley, poured out flames and sparks heavenward and cracked mockingly in the night air; and I saw mothers and maidens tearing their hair and shrieking to Heaven in the fright and despair, and little children, voiceless and tearless in the pitiable terror. I saw a beautiful girl, the daughter of a clergyman, standing in the front door of her home while its stable and outbuildings were burning, tearing the yellow tresses from her head, taking up and repeating the oaths of passing skirmishers and shrieking with wild laughter, for the horrors of the night had driven her mad...it is an insult to civilization and to God to pretend the Laws of War justify such warfare.[90]

Thus, Sheridan destroyed not only the economic and practical strength of the Valley but also, at least for the time, the Valley's spirit. Sheridan's report from Strasburg on October 7, 1864, gives a revealing account of the overwhelming extent of the destruction:

The grain and forage in advance of these points up to Staunton had previously been destroyed. In moving back to this point the whole country from the Blue Ridge to the North Mountains has been made untenable for a rebel army. I have destroyed over 2,000 barns filled with wheat, hay, and farming implements; over seventy mills filled with flour and wheat; have driven in front of the army over 4[000] head of stock, and have killed and issued to the troops not less than 3,000 sheep.... A large number of horses have been obtained, a proper estimate of which I cannot now make. Lieutenant John R. Meigh, my engineer officer, was murdered beyond Harrisonburg, near Dayton. For this atrocious act all the houses within an area of five miles were burned.... The people here are getting sick of the war; heretofore they have had no reason to complain, because they have been living in great abundance.... To-morrow I will continue the destruction of wheat, forage, etc., down to Fisher's Hill. When this is completed the Valley, from Winchester up to Staunton, ninety-two miles, will have but little in it for man or beast.... the grain and forage from Staunton to Strasburg had been left for the wintering of Early's army.[91]

Sheridan's tactics in the Shenandoah Valley, with the blessing of Ulysses S. Grant, achieved the desired objectives. Its people were demoralized, and its value as a source of sustenance for Early's forces (as well as for the rest of the Confederate army) was destroyed. Sheridan was delighted with the results and was convinced that "total war" was a necessary and justified means of combatting an enemy. In later years, he would use the same strategies against the Plains Indians:

Following the tactics he had employed in Virginia, Sheridan sought to strike directly at the material basis of the Plains Indian nations. He believed—correctly, it turned out—that attacking the Indians in their encampments during the winter would give him the element of surprise and take advantage of the scarce forage available for Indian mounts. He was unconcerned about the likelihood of high casualties among noncombatants, once remarking that "If a village is attacked and women and children killed, the responsibility is not with the soldiers but with the people whose crimes necessitated the attack."[92]

But the Plains Indians would have to wait. After the Burning, Sheridan had one more task to complete before leaving the Shenandoah Valley to the starving crows.

Chapter 4

THE BATTLE

*My men did not fight as I expected them to do...they were weak and
the enemy was strong.*

—Jubal Early

Although Waynesboro never witnessed the devastation experienced by
other Virginia communities, the battle that occurred at Waynesboro
in March 1865 was not the first time the peace and quiet of the small
village on the banks of the South River had been disturbed by the Civil
War. Waynesboro's first experience was little more than a close call, but one
that alarmed local citizens nonetheless. Confederate brigadier general John
D. Imboden was guarding Waynesboro as part of Union general David
Hunter's army left Staunton and marched toward Waynesboro on June
9 and 10, 1864. Imboden was also protecting the strategically important
Rockfish Gap (a quick route over the Blue Ridge to Lynchburg), the Blue
Ridge (Crozet) Tunnel and the Virginia Central Railroad. The citizens of
Waynesboro had good cause for their alarm. They had already heard of
what Hunter had done to Staunton, just a few days earlier. Hunter described
the damage inflicted in his official report:

> *At Staunton I destroyed a large amount of public stores, consisting of shoes,
> saddles, harness, and clothing, 3 cannon and about 1,000 stand of small-
> arms, also several extensive establishments for the manufacture of army
> clothing and equipments. I also had the Virginia Central Railroad entirely*

destroyed for several miles east and west of the town, burning all the depot buildings, shops, and warehouses belonging to the road. About 500 prisoners (for the most part wounded and invalids) fell into our hands here.[93]

Hunter's army even destroyed the presses and type of Staunton's pro-Union newspaper, the *Staunton Spectator.* The paper's publisher, Richard Mauzy, later wrote that Hunter "delighted in destroying the property of southern people." As they approached Waynesboro, Hunter's men overran and captured Confederate pickets but were repulsed by Imboden. Waynesboro was spared any damage.

Just a little more than three months later, on September 27, 1864, Union forces near Staunton were again sent to Waynesboro to destroy the railroad bridge and Blue Ridge Tunnel. But Confederate forces came from the area near Port Republic and successfully defended both the bridge and the tunnel. Joseph Waddell wrote of this skirmish:

The Federal army, some 3,000 men, under General Torbert, entered Staunton on Monday evening, September 26, and, passing through, camped on the Waynesborough road. A part of them went to Waynesborough on Tuesday, during which day the remainder of them occupied Staunton. They entered very few houses and committed no depredation of any consequence. They impressed all the negro men into their service, and took them down the railroad to destroy the track and bridges. The colored people were very indignant, and did much less damage to the railroad than they could have done.

On Wednesday, the 28th, the whole Federal command moved to Waynesborough, and late that evening they were attacked by a party of Confederate cavalry from Brown's Gap. The enemy were driven off, leaving about forty dead and more than eighty prisoners. They returned through Staunton late Wednesday night, in great haste and some disorder, and went down the Valley as they came up, by the Springhill road. They appeared to spend Thursday and Thursday night in burning barns in the direction of Middle river, the whole heavens being illuminated until a late hour.[94]

George Hawke provided additional detail about this incident:

On Wednesday, September 28 Wickham's cavalry and Pegram's infantry division came down from the Port Republic-Brown's Gap area over present Route 629, now discontinuous through Shenandoah National Park and south along the trail that became Route 340, and drove the Federals back to

Staunton. Waddell claims the Union forces lost 40 dead and more than 80 prisoners. If so, it was a heavy loss for such a small engagement.

The strike at Waynesboro did little damage to the railroad bridge, and Union forces did not reach the tunnel. Some supplies, cattle and food were destroyed or taken, and an unnamed mill set afire.[95]

Waynesborians no doubt prayed that they'd seen the last of war near their homes, but that was not to be. There would be one more incident before Lee's surrender at Appomattox.

Although Early's army would be the only real opposition that Sheridan would meet on his trek from Winchester to the James River Valley, the Battle of Waynesboro isn't remembered by most historians today as much of a battle when compared to other actions. Even so, Union captain Harlan Page Lloyd of the 22nd New York Cavalry made this observation about the engagement:

The Battle of Waynesboro, Virginia, was fought on the second day of March, 1865. Judged by the numbers engaged on either side, or by the number killed and wounded, it was not one of the great battles of the war. But it was a memorable battle in this, that it resulted in the capture of the last organized Confederate force in the Shenandoah Valley, a valley which, in one part or another, was one continuous battle-field from 1861–1865. It was important also in this, that it left General Sheridan free to move, with his two divisions of veteran cavalry, over the Blue Ridge, through the heart of Virginia, to march to the James region to rejoin our gallant comrades of the Army of the Potomac, and to take a leading part in that wonderful series of movements which culminated at Appomattox.[96]

Despite what may seem to be but a footnote in the history of the Civil War, the Battle of Waynesboro resulted in many of the same consequences seen in larger, longer and more evenly matched engagements. There were great acts of courage, self-sacrifice, death and close calls—some of these acts would call for monuments, and others have long since been forgotten. And despite what many view as an inconsequential engagement, the battle was a factor in what followed and how events ultimately led to the Confederacy's demise.

After Early successfully defended the strategically important city of Lynchburg from Union general David Hunter's army in June 1864, Lee ordered Early to threaten Washington—a move that Lee hoped would cause General Grant to divert troops from the Richmond-Petersburg lines. Lee's strategy worked, at least temporarily. But this success was then followed by Early's successive losses at Winchester, Fisher's Hill, Tom's Brook and Cedar Creek. Things got worse in December when Lee ordered three of Early's divisions to Petersburg. Further adding to Early's woes of a reduced, demoralized force was the fact that ordinarily sympathetic citizens had become dispirited and sick of the war. The drought of 1864 and the Burning that following fall meant that food was scarce and mere sustenance was a daily challenge, as historian Joseph Waddell noted: "At this usually abundant season of the year, people heretofore accustomed to live in luxury, are scuffling for the necessaries of life.... At Waynesborough, the other day, I drank at supper and breakfast 'rye coffee' without sugar."[97]

Waddell's last diary entry of 1864 reflected the spirits of many Valley residents: "The last night of a dreary year, full of wretchedness. Forage is very scarce, and many horses are dying."[98] The "dreary year," along with the colder than normal winter of 1864–65, left Early's men disheartened and ill-prepared for a battle. It is likely that those disheartened sentiments were best expressed in a January 29, 1865 diary entry by a soldier with Early's army, Private Henry Robinson Berkeley: "Men's spirits dull, gloomy and all are evidently hopeless, waiting for we know not what end."[99]

All this doom and gloom was magnified even further by the fact that Sheridan's army was numerically superior, well fed and better equipped. Private Berkeley no doubt further expressed the pessimism of many of his fellow Confederates with his February 28 entry: "We heard that the Yankee cavalry were coming up the Valley with a very large force, said to be 15,000 [sic] strong. We are only about 1500. I don't see how it is possible for us to contend against such great odds. Ordered to be ready to move at a moment's notice."[100]

Private Henry Robinson Berkeley, circa 1862. *Author's collection.*

The Yankees, having just come off a string of victories in the Valley, were emboldened by Sheridan's confident (though arguably callous) tactics toward civilian targets, as well as their knowledge that they lacked nothing in terms of supplies and weaponry. One Winchester woman described Sheridan's army as it marched past her house en route for one final battle with Early's army:

> *Sheridan had been months getting his army in thorough order—drilling and inspection had been going on daily for months, and his army was in magnificent trim when they started for Petersburg. I witnessed one of the grandest spectacles that can be imagined as they were leaving—20,000 [sic] cavalry passing our house four abreast, thoroughly equipped in every detail. Their horses, having been in winter quarters so long, had been fed high and curried and rubbed until their coats shone like satin. Each man had a new saddle, bridle, and red blanket, and all their accoutrements such as swords, belts, etc., shone like gold. It was a grand sight, requiring hours in passing.*[101]

Confederate brigadier general Wharton later described Sheridan's cavalry as "splendidly equipped."[102] The contrast in condition of the two armies—both physically and psychologically—could not have been starker.

As Sheridan's army, ten thousand strong, headed south out of Winchester on February 27, Early's remaining forces were still in winter camp at Fishersville near the Virginia Central Railroad. Harlan Lloyd wrote of breaking camp to head south:

Sheridan's army following Early up the Valley of the Shenandoah, by Alfred R. Waud, circa 1864–65. *Courtesy Library of Congress.*

Early on the morning of February 27, 1865, we broke camp, set fire to our huts, formed a marching column, and started up the valley pike with our faces southward, with the grim determination in the heart of every officer and every man to make that the last campaign, not only in the Shenandoah Valley, but of the war...Under wintry skies, with the snow lying in shrunken drifts by the roadside, and in great masses on the mountains, with a drizzling rain, which froze as it fell, the dark column stretched to its full length, and would slowly up the familiar pike. I can well imagine that each man's thoughts were busy with the past, from General Sheridan...to the humblest private in the ranks, who had marched up and down the old pike so often, that every stone, and stump, and tree had become as familiar as the face of a friend.[103]

The macadamized Valley pike (modern U.S. Route 11) made moving up[104] (south) through the Valley easy for Sheridan's forces. His only deterrent was a brief encounter with a small force of Confederate cavalry under the command of General Thomas L. Rosser, about seventeen miles north of Staunton at Mount Crawford. But the small Confederate detachment could do little but offer some delaying tactics that included setting a covered bridge on fire. Rosser, who likely had fewer than three hundred men, was little more than an annoyance against the advancing Union force of almost ten thousand men. Sheridan offered the following account in his official report:

On the morning of February 27, 1865, we marched from Winchester up the Valley pike, with five days' rations in haversacks, and fifteen days' rations of coffee, sugar, and salt in wagons, thirty pounds of forage on each horse, one wagon for division headquarters, eight ambulances, and our ammunition train; no other wagons, except a

Major General Thomas Lafayette Rosser.
Author's collection.

pontoon train of eight boats, were permitted to accompany the command. My orders were to destroy the Virginia Central Railroad, the James River Canal, capture Lynchburg if practicable, and then join Major-General Sherman wherever he might be found in North Carolina, or return to Winchester; but in joining General Sherman I must be governed by the position of affairs after the capture of Lynchburg.

The command was in fine condition, but the weather was very bad, as the spring thaw, with heavy rains, had already come on. The valley and surrounding mountains were covered with snow which was fast disappearing, putting all the streams nearly past fording…. The march was resumed at 6 o'clock on the morning of the 29ᵗʰ [March 1], through Harrisonburg and Mount Crawford, and camp pitched on Middle River at Cline's Mills. Guerrillas hovered around us during the march, and at Mount Crawford General Rosser, with 200 or 300 cavalry, attempted to burn the bridge over the Middle Fork of the Shenandoah, but did not succeed; two of Capehart's regiments swam the river above the bridge, charged Rosser and routed him, driving him rapidly to Cline's Mills, the advance pushing almost to Staunton; but few of the enemy were killed, 30 taken prisoners, and 20 ambulances and wagons, with their contents, were captured and destroyed; our loss was 5 men wounded.[105]

Riders brought the news of Mount Crawford to Early's headquarters in Staunton. Early had already ordered the town abandoned and all supplies removed. Upon first hearing of Sheridan leaving Winchester, Early acted promptly:

My own headquarters were at Staunton, but there were no troops at that place except a local provost guard, and a company of reserves, composed of boys under 18 years of age, which was acting under orders of the Conscript Bureau. Orders were therefore given for the immediate removal of all stores from that place.[106]

Early then rode to the camps at Fishersville and ordered General Gabriel Wharton and Colonel William Nelson to Waynesboro. The Confederates started arriving in Waynesboro the night of March 1, with one resident later stating that "soldiers camped for the night in the front yard, tearing down the fence to keep their fires going."[107]

The following morning, Sheridan arrived in Staunton, accompanied by a cold rain, and was confronted with a decision. He already had orders to continue southward to Lynchburg and eventually join General Sherman. But Early's position in Waynesboro presented Sheridan with an opportunity. Sheridan justified his decision in his personal memoirs:

I entered Staunton the morning of March 2, and finding that Early had gone to Waynesboro with his infantry and Rosser, the question at once arose whether I should continue my march to Lynchburg direct, leaving my adversary in my rear, or turn east and open the way through Rockfish Gap to the Virginia Central railroad and James River canal. I felt confident of the success of the latter plan, for I knew that Early numbered not more than two thousand men; so, influenced by this…I directed Merritt to move toward that place with Custer, to be closely followed by Devin.[108]

Sheridan would not find the road to Waynesboro as welcoming as the macadamized Valley Pike. Early's men and wagons had already made a bad road worse, and the rain and melting snow only added to the miserable condition of the Staunton Pike (modern U.S. Route 250), making it almost impassable. Wagons would sink to the axle and horses to their bellies. Sheridan noted the condition of the road to Waynesboro: "The by-roads were miry beyond description, rain having fallen almost incessantly since we left Winchester, but notwithstanding the down-pour the column pushed on, men and horses almost unrecognizable from the mud covering them from head to foot."[109]

As already noted, Early would be at a severe disadvantage—numerically and otherwise—as the Battle of Waynesboro commenced in the afternoon of March 2, 1865. The exact makeup of Early's forces is difficult to ascertain, as there are no official reports from the Confederate side. There are, however,

Sheridan's wagon trains in the Shenandoah Valley, early morning, October 1864, by Alfred R. Waud. *Courtesy Library of Congress.*

numerous recountings in memoirs and diaries. And it comes as no surprise that the numbers and specifics from the various sources do not all agree. The sources suggest total Confederate numbers ranging from 1,200 to 2,000. Some of that number may have included Confederates already in or near Waynesboro but not attached to Early's army. Early himself would later allude to that possibility as an explanation for the discrepancies. Jennings Cropper Wise wrote the following in his history of the artillery in the Army of Northern Virginia:

> *Col. Nelson with six pieces of his battalion remained with Early.... Two very small brigades of Wharton's Division, and Nelson's artillery command now comprised Early's whole force, which was placed in camp near Fishersville between Staunton and Waynesborough.*[110]

In Early's own account after the war, he wrote, "The last report for Wharton's command showed 1200 men for duty; but, as it was exceedingly inclement, and raining and freezing, there were not more than 1000 muskets on the line, and Nelson had six pieces of artillery."[111] Early would point out that "a very considerable number of recently exchanged and paroled prisoners were at the time in the valley, on leave of absence from General Lee's army."[112] This could offer some explanation for the conflicting numbers.

Michal P. West also noted in his regimental history of the 30th Battalion Virginia Sharpshooters that Wharton later reported that he had "only 912 effective men" on the day before the battle.[113]

General Gabriel Wharton was a native Virginian and graduated second from Virginia Military Institute in 1847. He would command two small brigades at Waynesboro. First appointed a major in the 45th Virginia Infantry, he took command of the 51st Virginia on July 17, 1861, and was promoted to colonel. Wharton was a respected and seasoned veteran, and Early assigned him the unenviable task of holding the Confederates' threadbare line against the Federal assault. Harlan Lloyd would pay a soldier's tribute to General Wharton: "Wharton's division, though reduced in numbers, was the same steady body of brave and determined men, whom we had encountered so often in previous years, and the Confederacy had no better."[114]

Composing the Confederate infantry under the command Wharton were two small brigades. The limited information available shows that Colonel Augustus Forsberg led soldiers from the 50th and 51st Virginia and the 30th Battalion Sharpshooters. Colonel Thomas Smith's Brigade was made up of men from the 36th and 60th Regiments, as well as the 45th Battalion. Historian Richard

General Gabriel Wharton. *Courtesy Virginia Military Institute Archives.*

Nicholas added that "there may also have been a company of the Valley Reserves. In all, there were probably no more than 1,000 to 1,200 infantrymen."[115]

Early would depend largely on Lieutenant Colonel William Nelson's six-gun artillery battalion to discourage a frontal assault and, Early hoped, bluff Sheridan into a stalemate. Jennings Wise described Nelson:

> [C]*losely connected by blood with Lee, Pendleton, Page, Braxton, Carter, and many other officers of the Artillery,* [he] *was a picturesque character. Among the first to raise a battery in the spring of 1861, he had gradually risen to high rank...he was not noted for dash, nor was he by training a soldier. But he possessed an unblemished character, was sternly courageous, as dependable as any officer in the Army, and was adored by his men who regarded him as a father.*[116]

Nelson was born the same year as Robert E. Lee (1807) and resided at the birthplace of Thomas Nelson Page, Oakland, all his life. He was an interesting character and, as already noted, had deeply rooted ties to Old Virginia. Historian William H. Runge offered the following description of Nelson:

> *A pious churchman, he was noted for his sincerity, kindness, and strictness in matters of discipline. He was a superb horseman and continued to ride strenuously up to the time of his death in 1892 at the age of eighty-five. Several times during the war he had his horse shot out from under him. Though he had not the soldier's dashing, reckless nature, as did so many of his contemporaries, he could always be spotted by his silk top hat which he wore even on the battlefield.... Robin Berkeley recorded in his diary that, later in the war, most of the men "learned to know him better and to love*

and admire his stern courage and noble qualities of mind and heart, and were ready to follow him wherever he might lead.".…Nelson was in action without interruption for the length of the war though men much younger were not able to stand the strain. In his "Burial of the Guns," Thomas Nelson Page modeled the "Old Colonel" after his uncle, Colonel Nelson, and in this story is much of the flavor of the old gentleman's character. The "Old Colonel" died on a Sunday morning in 1892, while kneeling at his bed in prayer.[117]

Composing Nelson's battalion were the Amherst Battery (Captain Thomas J. Kirkpatrick), the Fluvanna Battery (Captain Charles G. Snead) and the Georgia Regular Battery (Captain John Milledge Jr.).[118]

The only other Confederate aid would come from General Thomas Lafayette Rosser. Another native Virginian, Rosser was known as a daring and capable cavalry officer. But after many of his men were furloughed due to lack of forage from the drought and Sheridan's Burning the previous year, Rosser was only able to round up roughly one hundred men.

Harlan Lloyd viewed the potential capture of Rosser—as well as Early—particularly desirable: "Rosser was the classmate of General Custer at West Point, and our frequent encounters with him and his men made us feel that we would rather capture Early and Rosser than any other two men in the Confederate army."[119]

Rosser and George Armstrong Custer were actually roommates and became good friends while at West Point. Originally born in Campbell County, Virginia, Rosser spent his teen years in Texas, where his family moved when he was thirteen. Rosser would be introduced to the Civil War by commanding a company at the battle of First Manassas. He would be promoted to colonel of the 5th Virginia Cavalry at the Seven Days Campaign and then brigadier general after Gettysburg.

Against Early's scant force was arrayed a comparatively massive Union army with equally capable and seasoned commanders. Early was, of course, more than aware of his diminished capabilities due to the severely reduced number of men under his command. One incident told after the war involving Early and Confederate general Richard Ewell illustrates that Early, ironically, placed a high priority on numbers. While attending a church service at Orange Courthouse, Early sat and listened as a regiment chaplain drew "the ghastly picture of a sinner's death" and asked those assembled that if all the dead soldiers of the war could be "summoned up…how would you receive it?" Early is alleged to have leaned over to Ewell and whispered, "I'd conscript the last one of them!"[120]

General George Armstrong Custer, circa 1865. *Courtesy Library of Congress.*

Sheridan's lieutenants included Major General Wesley Merritt, chief of cavalry. A West Pointer, Merritt would serve as a commissioner at the surrender of Lee's army at Appomattox.

Brigadier General Thomas C. Devin would command the 1st Cavalry Division, consisting of 5,047 men, and Companies C and E, 4th U.S. Artillery, consisting of 54 men. Before the Civil War, Devin had served several years as a New York militia officer and quickly became respected as an able cavalryman. After once quizzing Devin about cavalry maneuvers, Brigadier General John Buford proclaimed, "I can't teach Col. Devin anything about cavalry; he knows more about the tactics than I do!"[121]

Commanding the 3rd Cavalry Division, consisting of 4,840 men, and Company M, 2nd U.S. Artillery, consisting of 46 men, was Major General

George Armstrong Custer. The flamboyant Custer remains, to this day, one of the most recognizable names in American military history. Graduating last in his class at West Point, he redeemed himself to history during the Civil War—only to suffer a historic defeat at the hands of Lakota and Cheyenne Indian warriors at the Battle of the Little Bighorn.

Harlan Lloyd gave us a more detailed—as well as admiring—description of Sheridan's command and army:

General Thomas C. Devin, by Mathew Brady, circa 1860–65. *Courtesy National Archives.*

> *The chief of cavalry was General Wesley Merritt, an able and accomplished soldier, who had been a successful brigade commander during the previous war, and later had commanded the First Division. General Thomas C. Devin succeeded to the command of the First Division. The First Brigade was commanded by Colonel [Peter] Stagg, the Second Brigade by Colonel [Charles L.] Fitzhugh, and the Reserve Brigade by General Alfred Gibbs.*
>
> *The Third Cavalry Division was under the command of General George A. Custer, next to Sheridan the idol of the cavalry corps, the dashing, brave, and successful chevalier, a born master of the horse, and ideal leader of cavalry, a genial and accomplished gentleman.*
>
> *His first brigade was commanded by Colonel [Alexander] Pennington, the Second Brigade by General William Wells, and his Third Brigade, which had been sent to us from the Army of West Virginia, was commanded by Colonel [Henry] Capehart. My regiment, the Twenty-second New York Cavalry, was in the Second Brigade of the Third Division.*[122]

Lloyd then provided some insight as to how some Union soldiers viewed Sheridan's Valley Campaign:

I had been wounded in one of the fights in the valley several months before. I had at this time an open wound, and was really in no physical condition for field service, especially in a winter campaign. But I felt sure that we were about to enter upon the last struggle of the war, and I was determined to be in at the death.[123]

Harlan's determination and confidence in his fellow soldiers offered, once again, an illustration of the stark contrast between the physical and psychological conditions of the two armies:

No finer body of men ever rode forth than those bronzed veterans of the cavalry corps. They were the men who had fought under [Major General George] Stoneman, and afterward under [General Alfred] Pleasanton at Aldie, at Chancellorsville, and at Gettysburg. They had fought under Sheridan at the Wilderness, at Trevillian, and at Cold Harbor.... They were men who had known in their campaigns, on distant fields, both successes and failure. But for them, the Valley of the Shenandoah had always been lighted with the bonfires

Rose Hall, the Gallaher home, circa 1945. *Courtesy Waynesboro Public Library.*

of victory…in regard to the valley campaign of 1864, what had never been said by any other in the land, that it had literally captured every piece of cannon whose fire had been directed against it. All the troopers were bold, rough riders. It was a conspicuous example of the survival of the fittest, and there was no man in the company at that time who could not be depended upon in any emergency, and to the last extremity.[124]

Early's army had marched into Waynesboro during the night of March 1 and the early morning hours of March 2. Early and some of his staff took breakfast at the Gallaher home, Rose Hall. DeWitt Gallaher wrote in his diary that he saw Early "turn down a tumbler full of whiskey before breakfast," adding, "This was a weakness of his."[125]

The Union army's march from Staunton was slow, inhibited by the mud and deplorable condition of the road. But Custer's 3rd Cavalry division, followed by Devin's 1st Cavalry division, slogged on. Next in line were the 2nd and 4th Artillery units, comprising twelve pieces, sixteen ammunition wagons, forty-three supply wagons, approximately one hundred mules, eight ambulances and eight pontoons. The additional traffic on the already rut-filled road caused its condition to worsen with each step.

Harlan Page Lloyd described the march to Waynesboro:

Through rain, and sleet, and hail, and storm, through mud which rendered the roads almost impassable, through streams without bridges, we pushed on with an eagerness inspired by the hope of capturing Early, the route running near the present track of the Chesapeake and Ohio Rail road, from Staunton eastward through Fisherville [sic] to Waynesboro.[126]

Lloyd noted that members of the 22nd New York Cavalry ran into a Confederate rear guard soon after departing Staunton: "A sharp skirmish ensued, and the rebels fled to Fisherville [sic]."[127]

Custer's official report noted the following:

On the 2d we moved to Staunton, where the command was halted for a short interval. In accordance with verbal orders received from the major-general commanding the expedition I then marched toward Waynesborough. My orders were to proceed to Waynesborough, ascertain something definite in regard to the position, movements, and strength of the enemy, and, if possible, to destroy the railroad bridge over the South River at that point. The roads were almost impassable, owing to the mud caused by the heavy rains of the past few days. Our march was necessarily slow. Upon reaching Fishersville, six miles from Staunton, our advance struck the enemy's pickets, and drove them in the direction of Waynesborough. Upon arriving at the latter point we found the enemy in force, posted behind a formidable line of earth-works. His position was well chosen, being upon a range of hills west of the town, from which his artillery could command all the approaches, while his infantry could, by their fire, sweep the open space extending along their entire front.[128]

It is interesting that Custer opined that Early's position was "well-chosen," as others, including those in Early's command, would later criticize Early's choice. General Rosser had advised Early to take up a position on the opposite (east) bank of the South River, but Early rejected this counsel. He chose, instead, to back Wharton's vastly outnumbered infantry division up against the rain-swollen river. Should the Confederates find it necessary to retreat and escape, there would be no easy route. The ford and footbridge from Main Street leading to Rockfish Gap would ultimately be blocked on the east side of the river by some members of the 8th New York, and a railroad bridge—laid with wooden planks and offering only a narrow

Main Street, Waynesboro, Virginia, circa 1890. Although this image comes decades later, the landscape on Main Street would have been very similar in 1865. *Courtesy Waynesboro Heritage Foundation.*

escape route—was not enough space to handle 1,200 men rushing to avoid a slaughter. Another footbridge that existed at the time, and was farther upriver and closer to the battle, was apparently flooded.

Confederate mapmaker Captain Jedediah Hotchkiss expressed his criticism later in his journal: "The general committed an unpardonable error in posting so small a force with a swollen river in its rear and with its flanks wholly exposed."[129] Hotchkiss also noted the lack of escape options: "The only precaution taken was to have boards put on the railroad bridge for a foot bridge in the morning. The only other crossing was a foot bridge by the roadside, two or three feet wide."[130] After the war, General Wharton would echo Hotchkiss's criticism, and Colonel Augustus Forsberg, who was in command of one of Wharton's brigades, would write in his memoirs: "Many a longing eye was cast towards the mountain gap [Rockfish] only two miles in our rear where we could have defied General Sheridan's whole army."[131]

Early had his defenses in position stretched along a northeast–southwest line that would coincide roughly along present-day Pine Avenue in the residential area known as the Tree Streets. Early's right stretched beyond Main Street to the north across the railroad tracks, with at least one piece of artillery on the high ground between present-day Florence Avenue and Port Republic Road. His left flank ended somewhere between present-day 14th Street and 15th Street—about a quarter mile from the banks of the South River lying to the south. Early's left flank ended in an area known today as Forest Hill and known in 1865 as Gallaher's Woods (owned by the same prominent Waynesboro family who owned Rose Hall). Several of the massive oaks still standing today would have witnessed the battle 150 years ago. Early had five more pieces of his artillery facing west on the high ground running along Pine Avenue. Although some writers have suggested that the Confederates did not construct trenches, there is physical evidence (as well as observations from Union soldiers) that they actually did. They also tore down a fence and used the rails to construct a crude barricade in front of the hastily dug trenches.

At first glance, these positions would seem ideal to defend against the Federals advancing from the west. But Early was legitimately criticized by his fellow officers for choosing this location due to the fact that the South River (roughly a half mile directly behind the Confederate line) was, as previously noted, swollen and would be difficult—if not impossible—to ford in a hasty retreat. But Early would later defend his choice of position:

Present-day Pine Avenue, Waynesboro, Virginia. *Photo by author.*

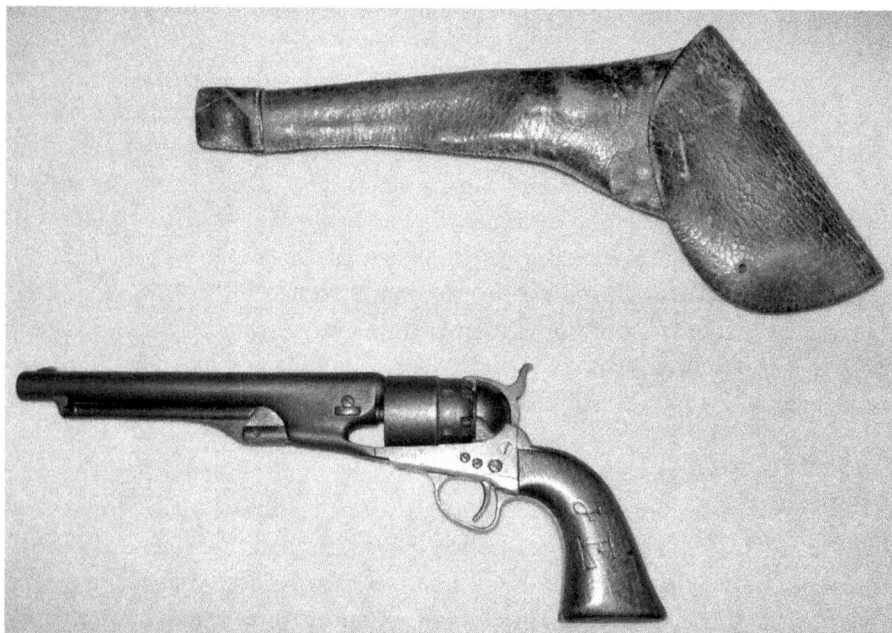

Jubal Early's pistol. *Photo by author.*

My object in taking this position was to secure the removal of five pieces of artillery for which there were no horses, and some stores still in Waynesboro, as well as to present a bold front to the enemy, and ascertain the object of his movement, which I could not do very well if I took refuge at once in the mountain…. I did not intend making my final stand on this ground, yet I was satisfied that if my men would fight, which I had no reason to doubt, I could hold the enemy in check until night, and then cross the river and take position in Rock-fish Gap; for I had done more difficult things than that during the war.[132]

Harlan Page Lloyd also acknowledged that Early's position had, at least, some advantages:

Early had seized the salient points of the elevation west of the town, had erected earthworks, and planted his artillery so as to sweep, by a concentrated fire, the only road leading to his position; while the open fields in his front were so soft with the heavy rains and upheaving frosts that he deemed them utterly impassable for cavalry. These fields constituted a deep, miry mass of mud…. He had a very quick eye for the advantage of a position, and he could arrange an army with marvelous skill. His position at Waynesboro was carefully chosen, and his force admirably arranged for defense. His only mistake was in his over-confidence. He threw his left flank so far to the front, in the hope of sweeping with an infantry fire the entire open space intervening between his position and the woods on the west, that he neglected to protect the flank by refusing its extreme wing.[133]

Lloyd provided further detail of Early's line and command:

General Long commanded the right wing, General Wharton the left, while Nelson's artillery was in the center behind hastily-constructed breast works, with the guns so placed as to sweep the fields. Rosser's cavalry was on the extreme rebel right to protect it from a flank movement by way of the railroad track.[134]

Early may well have reasoned that the open, muddy fields in front of his defenses would serve as a quagmire and natural defense, possibly resulting in a standoff. But if the Union army did attempt a direct assault, the terrain would slow them down and expose them to deadly artillery fire. That logic almost worked.

Looking west from where the Confederate line was (from what is today Pine Avenue). Although this photograph dates to circa 1906, the landscape would have been very similar to what the Confederates would have seen in 1865, except for the fact that more of it would have been wooded. *Courtesy Waynesboro Heritage Foundation.*

Regardless of the reasoning, the shivering, sleet-covered Confederates had the unenviable posture of having almost ten thousand[135] Yankees in front of them and a swollen, cold river behind them. There was also another problem with the Confederates' position. Early had failed to extend his left flank far enough to the south (toward present-day 16th Street) so that it would anchor at the river. This left his left flank exposed, a weakness that would give the Union army a crucial key to its quick victory.

Louisa (Lou) Withrow (sister of Colonel Charles Withrow of General Rosser's staff) was teaching grammar school in a building on Main Street, just a few city blocks from Early's line, when the battle began. She would later write, "I was teaching one morning when a battle was being fought, just above our town toward Fishersville. I had so much of the stick-to-itive [*sic*] in my nature that I did not dismiss the school, till I heard the roar of the cannon."[136]

Private Henry Robinson Berkeley, who was manning the artillery piece anchoring Early's right flank, described the ominous gathering he witnessed as the battle was about to unfold:

> [T]*he weather was cold and rainy. We took a position on a very high hill, north of Waynesboro, on the Port Republic Road. After remaining here until three in the evening in a cold and sleety rain and being nearly frozen, the Yankee cavalry, in a large and heavy body, forming almost a semicircle, appeared in front and on both flanks.*[137]

Above: Lou Withrow headstone, Riverview Cemetery, Waynesboro, Virginia. *Photo by author.*

Right: Cover of Lou Withrow's "Reminisces." *Courtesy Waynesboro Heritage Foundation.*

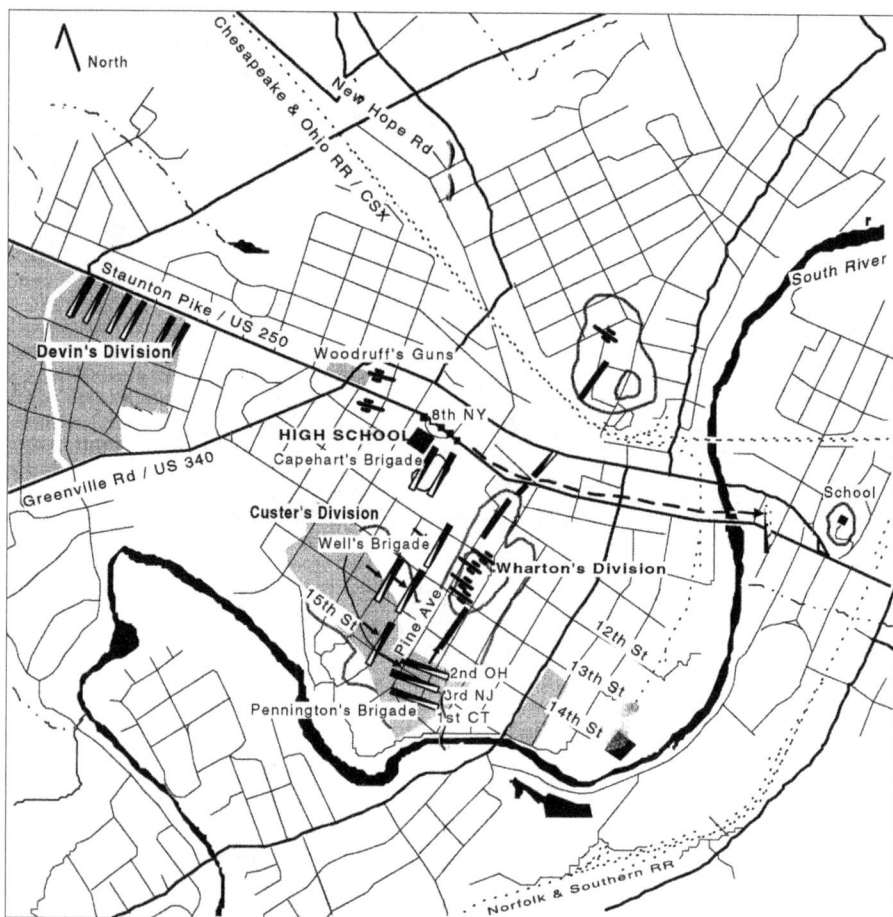

Battle of Waynesboro battlefield, created by Collier Mapping, Bridgewater, Virginia. The map is based on Major Gillespie's 1873 map of the battlefield. *Used by permission.*

Jed Hotchkiss would later write the following recollection of the commencement of the battle, as well as the positioning[138] of the Confederate artillery:

> *Wharton's division was put in line of battle at an early hour at Waynesborough, the left at the edge of the woods northwest of town, and the right at the barn back of Gallagher's [sic], with two pieces of artillery on the right, one just in rear and near the railroad and one more to the right on the river road. After the enemy advanced, four pieces were taken to the left wing and disposed along it. About 2 p.m. the enemy came on and formed a*

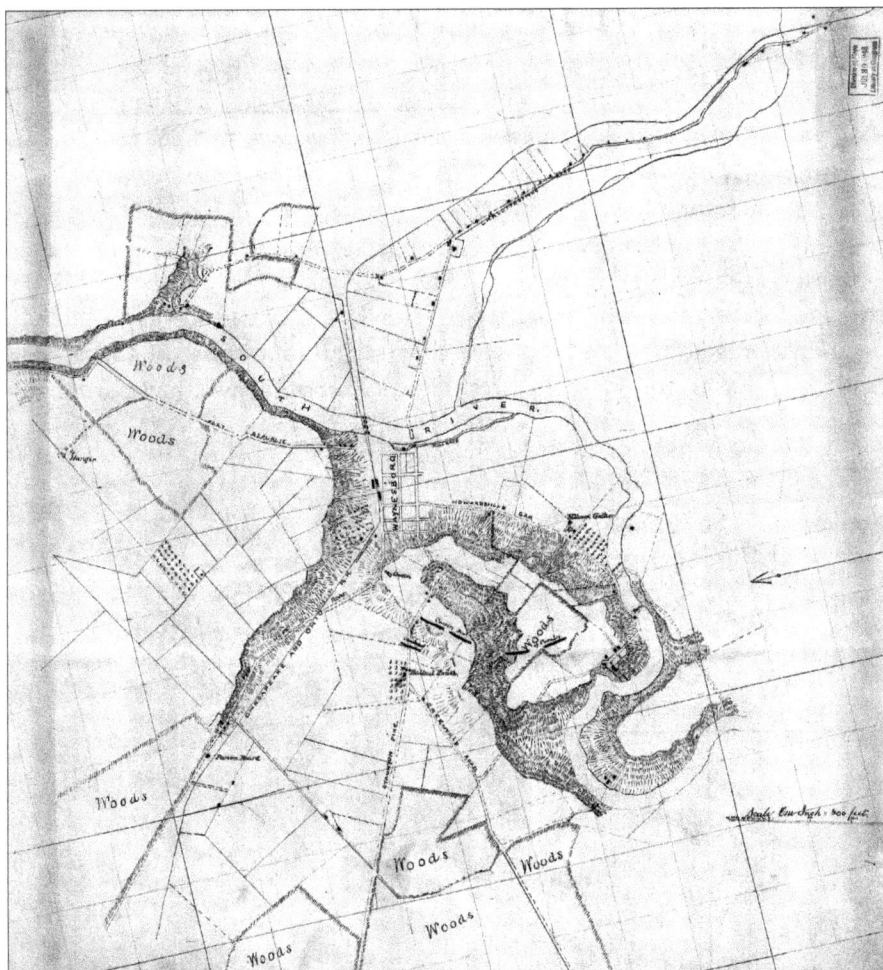

Preliminary battle map of Waynesboro, Virginia, March 2, 1865, by Jedediah Hotchkiss. *Courtesy Library of Congress.*

line of battle about a mile in front of Waynesborough and on the right of the road, deploying skirmishers along our front and to the left. We opened artillery on them, especially from our left, and did them some damage, compelling them to fall back and breaking their line, and it seemed from appearances through the sleet that they were falling back. [139]

Harlan Lloyd would later describe his memory of the beginning of the battle:

The Twenty-second New York was immediately deployed in a skirmish line and engaged the rebel infantry which was thrown out in front, and drove it back within the earthworks. This regiment was ordered to hold its position until the remainder of the brigade and division could come up. Riding back rapidly, I reported the situation to General Wells, who ordered me to ride at once to General Custer giving him the same information.[140]

Custer then ordered Brigadier General William Wells to send his 2nd Brigade forward in support of the 22nd New York. Early must have initially been encouraged by what he observed. The natural defense of the muddy fields in front of the Confederates' elevated position was hampering the

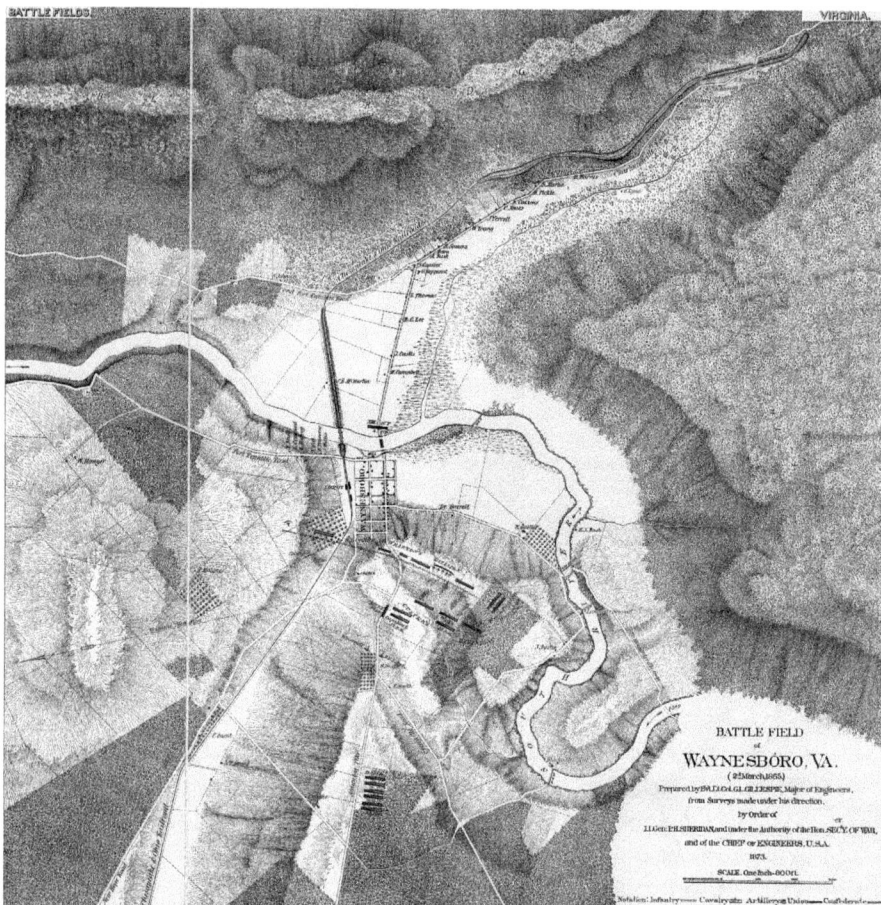

Battlefield of Waynesboro, Virginia, prepared by Brevet Lieutenant Colonel G.L. Gillespie, major of engineers, 1873. *Courtesy Library of Congress.*

Union army's frontal attack. Harlan Lloyd wrote, "The rebel artillery was firing rapidly, and our skirmish line was so completely mired in the mud that it was difficult either to advance or retreat."[141]

The sight of the Yankees getting bogged down in the muddy fields below his lines must have been encouraging to Early. That feeling would be short-lived. Encountering the stiff resistance from the Confederates, Custer considered other options. He quickly discovered the gap in the Southerners' left flank. He would later report:

> *The Second Brigade, Col. [sic] Wells commanding, was at once moved against the enemy to compel him to display his force. A short but brisk engagement convinced me that while our success would be doubtful, it would involve a large loss of life to attack the enemy in his front. A careful reconnaissance along his entire line convinced me that the enemy had a heavy force of infantry behind his works, while ten [sic] pieces of artillery were in position and completely covered his front. But one point seemed favorable for attack. The enemy's left flank, instead of resting on South River, was thrown well forward, leaving a short gap between his left and the river. The approach to this point could be made under cover of the woods. I directed Lieut.-Col. Whitaker, of my staff, to conduct three regiments of Pennington's brigade to our extreme right.*[142]

There are conflicting accounts as to how Custer discovered the gap on Early's left. Harlan Lloyd credited Custer's "keen eye":

> *The weak point in Early's position was, that General Wharton's left flank did not extend to and rest upon South River, as it should have done. The keen eye of Custer quickly discovered this vulnerable point, and his plan was instantly made to turn the left flank of the rebel position, while a vigorous attack was made in front.*[143]

But in a 1923 *Confederate Veteran* magazine article, DeWitt Clinton Gallaher claimed that Custer's discovery was aided by Confederate deserters:

> *Two boys, deserters from the vicinity (whose names were well known and which I withhold), and who for some months had been with Sheridan, guided Custer, concealed by the woods on Early's left flank above referred to, to a sunken lane leading from the Greenville road to the South River ford, and wholly unprotected by Early on his extreme left flank.*[144]

Regardless, Custer exploited the breach masterfully. He ordered Lieutenant Colonel Whitaker, along with three of Pennington's regiments from the brigade, to the Union army's extreme right. The Federals, armed with breech-loading, seven-shot Spencer carbine repeating rifles, were ordered to dismount. There they were, according to Custer's official report, "held in readiness," facing the southern terminus of Early's left flank and concealed in the woods. At the same time, General Wells, in command of the 2nd Brigade, was ordered to threaten the enemy in front by "displaying a heavy force of mounted skirmishers." And Colonel Capehart, in command of the 3rd Brigade, was "ordered to place his brigade in readiness to charge the enemy in front the moment the attack on the right began." The two remaining regiments of the 1st Brigade were given similar orders.[145]

In order to deceive Early, Custer first ordered Woodruff's horse artillery to the rear, in plain view of the Confederates. They were then moved back to the front, also under the cover of woods, and were in position to be able to fire on the Confederate line. Pennington's men then approached the Confederates' left flank along a low-lying road through what is today Ridgeview Park. Climbing a steep embankment at the southern end of present-day Pine and Locust Avenues, they surprised the Confederates. Custer described the results of his plan:

> *At a given signal the three dismounted regiments* [Pennington's brigade: 2nd Ohio, 3rd New Jersey and 1st Connecticut] *charged on our right. Woodruff opened his guns upon the enemy, compelling them to lie down behind their works, while the brigades of Wells and Capehart moved to the attack in front, at the charge. So sudden was our attack and so great was the enemy's surprise that but little time was offered for resistance.*[146]

Early's men, bearing single-shot muzzle-loaders, could not match the deadly firepower of the Spencers. Often referred to as "seven shooters," Confederate soldiers understandably dreaded facing an opponent who could fire twenty rounds per minute to his three. By the time of the Battle of Waynesboro, the Spencer carbine's reputation had become well established as to both its technological superiority on a battlefield and the psychological impact it bore on soldiers on both sides of an engagement. This was noted by Union general James H. Wilson in a letter to Brigadier General Alexander B. Dyer dated January 2, 1865:

Confederate flag captured at the Battle of Waynesboro. This regimental Confederate battle flag was captured by Private Michael Crowley, Company A, 22nd New York Volunteer Cavalry. It was manufactured by the Staunton clothing depot in Staunton, Virginia, in late 1864 to supply the Valley army. The entire lower third of the flag was soaked in the blood of its bearer, causing its eventual decay. Crowley was awarded the Medal of Honor for the capture of this flag. *Courtesy Museum of the Confederacy.*

There is no doubt that the Spencer carbine is the best fire-arm yet put into the hands of the soldier, both for economy of ammunition and maximum effect physical and moral [sic]. Our best officers estimate one man armed with it equivalent to three of any other arm. I have never seen anything else like the confidence inspired by it in the regiments or brigades which have it. A common belief amongst them is if their flanks are covered they can go anywhere. I have seen a large number of dismounted charges made with them against cavalry, infantry, and breast-works, and never knew one to fail.[147]

Stephen Starr quoted what Union cavalryman Roger Hannaford was told by one of the Confederate prisoners taken at Waynesboro:

[I]t was useless to stand against our seven shooters…to see us coming at a run, never stopping to load, but running & firing… "Beside[s], you came with such a rush, so different from an infantry charge…" said an Officer, "the men are really afraid of the seven shooters, they dread them, a panic seems to possess them as soon as they see them coming."[148]

And panic is exactly what happened. The surprise flanking move and the sight of the Spencers was more than the demoralized Confederates could handle. Outmanned, outgunned, soaking wet and nearly frozen, the panicked Southerners offered only token resistance. As Jedediah Hotchkiss would later describe it, "[M]oving through the woods turned our left flank, which made a feeble resistance and give way, followed by the giving way of the whole line, and one of the most terrible panics and stampedes I have ever seen."[149]

While the left flank was collapsing, Union colonel Capehart's 3rd Brigade tore into the Confederate's front line; as local historian and author Robert Moore wrote, the Confederates fired a "single ragged volley."[150]

Harlan Lloyd gave a detailed description of what he witnessed as the Union army routed the Confederates:

> [W]*ith orders that when in position a signal should be given, so that a simultaneous attack might commence in front…we were scarcely in position when Custer's bugles, which had been trained to sound no other notes but those of the charge, rang out sharp and clear, and we started along that muddy road to make the last fight of the Shenandoah. What a wild ride that was! The condition of the road was past description. We started at full gallop, with the mud and water flying in every direction, and our movement was the signal for the rebel artillerists to concentrate their fire upon the narrow road along which we were hurrying. In a moment the shot and shell came tearing through our ranks, splashing the mud and water even worse than the horses had already done; and the Eighth New York soon presented the appearance of men who had been soaked bodily in the soft mire of the road. A shell struck a few feet in front of my horse and exploded as it struck. I felt a sharp concussion on the left side of my head, which almost stunned me, and for a moment I supposed I had been hit with a piece of the exploding shell. With an instinctive movement I put up my hand, and was relieved to find that it was not obdurate iron, but a plaster of soft mud driven with great rapidity, unpleasant, but not dangerous. It was not a time or place for one to be fastidious about his toilet; and, allowing the horses to choose their footing for themselves, we galloped up to the Confederate breastworks, sabers in hand, with ringing cheers rode down the artillerists, stopped the firing of their guns, crowded through the lines of the infantry, and into the town, hoping to capture General Early at his headquarters.[151]*

In his autobiography, Early wrote that he became aware of the Union's flanking movement on his left, writing:

> *I discovered a force moving to the left. I immediately sent a messenger with notice of this fact to General Wharton, who was on that flank, and with orders for him to look out and provide for the enemy's advance; and*

another messenger, with notice to the guns on the left, and directions for them to fire towards the advancing force, which could not be seen from where they were.[152]

Wharton was, at that same time, already en route to consult with Early. As soon as he rode up, Early "pointed out to him the disorder in his line, and ordered him to ride immediately to that point and rectify it."[153] But it was too little too late. Early noted, "Before he got back, the troops gave way on the left, after making very slight resistance, and soon everything was in a state of confusion and the men commenced crossing the river."[154]

Even with what should have been realized as an obvious rout, Early attempted to rally his men by racing to the South River: "I rode across it myself to try and stop them at the bridge and check the enemy; but they could not be rallied, and the enemy forded the river above and got in our rear. I now saw that everything was lost."[155]

Although Early's left flank collapsed, William Nelson's artillery battalion did not give up so easily—something of which Custer took special notice: "The artillery, however, continued to fire till the last moment and till our troops had almost reached the muzzles of their guns. One piece was captured with the sponge-staff still inserted in the bore and the charge rammed half way home."[156]

Henry Robinson Berkeley made the following entry in his diary regarding his part in the artillery firing: "I aimed and fired my gun five or six times that day. It looks now, as if they would be the last shots fired by the Confederate artillery in the Valley of Virginia."[157] Berkeley also wrote of his attempt to escape, as well as his disgust with Wharton's men:

We had only one little narrow plank over the [Virginia Central] railroad bridge by which we could retreat and it took so long to get over, that Custer's Yankee Brigade got ahead of us, and [did so] by a circular movement and by crossing a ford above the town. Wharton's two regiments behaved very badly and ran very disgracefully. Had they stood firm, we could have gotten back in the cover of the mountain and defended ourselves against Sheridan's whole 15,000 [sic]. I was captured after I had gotten over the railroad bridge in a little piece of oak woods to the left of the railroad as you come east.[158]

Berkeley further noted that his captors "treated us very well" but that they "could outswear any set of men I ever heard and were the most profane set I ever was so unfortunate as to be thrown with."[159]

Dr. Hunter McGuire, circa 1862. *Courtesy Virginia Military Institute Archives.*

Early and his staff, including General Wharton and Dr. Hunter McGuire, made a dash for the bridge that led out of town and toward the Blue Ridge Mountains. Early and Wharton escaped, but as Dr. McGuire's horse made a valiant effort to jump a rail fence, the two went tumbling into the mud. DeWitt Clinton Gallaher recounted the incident in his diary:

> He told me he was trying to escape and had reached a piece of woods, where the "Brandon" Hotel now stands in Basic, and finding his pursuers very close behind him tried to jump his horse over a low rail fence and get into the woods. But alas! His horse fell with him! An officer told the fellow to put his gun down, saying "He's MY prisoner." The Dr. told me he was a Mason and that he made a Masonic sign and the Yankee officer being a Mason also had saved his life. He said the enemy treated him very nicely and paroled him.[160]

McGuire's capture worked to the benefit of the Gallaher family—also explained in Gallaher's diary:

> I noticed a big fire and a column of smoke right in a line with my mother's house, which I supposed was burning. I afterwards found out the fire was from burning a lot of Early's wagons on the hill in front of Shaws (now Antrim's) house on the hill. Phil Coiner and I decided to ride into or as near as we could to Waynesboro. As we entered the town the last of the Yankees were leaving en-route to Charlottesville. I went home and got something to eat and listened to all that the Yankees had done while there. They (Hun like) had broken into my mother's smoke house, taken her hams, etc., broken into her pantry on her back

porch and taken almost everything they could find. However, some edibles were saved by the following incident. Dr. Hunter McGuire of Stonewall Jackson's old staff, but now of General Early's staff, and chief surgeon was captured by the enemy and asked to be paroled and allowed to go to my mother's. Being a non-combatant, and of very high rank he was allowed to go. He brought with him a staff officer of Sheridan's and my mother had them a nice meal prepared. While doing so, she came in and appealed to the Yankee Staff Officer, Lieut. [Charles Henry] Vail, for protection. He at once gave her a guard and drove the thieving rascals off.[161]

McGuire's membership in the Masons wasn't the only Masonic association that proved beneficial to the Gallahers during the battle. The patriarch of the family, Hugh Gallaher, was also a Mason, and this afforded the Gallaher family and their property additional protection:

My mother and children all hid in the cellar under our kitchen during the fighting. Fourteen of our men surrendered on our back porch where they had run when the stampede began. He also told me that while he and his Yankee protector were in our sitting room waiting for their meal, which my mother was preparing (for our negroes had been sent away except one woman, Mammy Jane), the Yankee officer noticed a Knight Templar picture on the wall. It had my father's name on it. He inquired who this Hugh L. Gallaher was? When told he said, of course, he would protect his family and did. He also stopped their plundering and burning down at the Tanyard nearby.[162]

Other battle participants weren't so fortunate. During the mêlée of the Confederate retreat through downtown Waynesboro and at the bottom of Main Street Hill, Colonel William H. Harman was surrounded by five Federals. There are conflicting reports as to what happened next. Several reports suggest that Harman refused to surrender and drew his sidearm in a brave attempt to escape. In doing so, he was gunned down. An article appearing in the October 31, 1949 issue of the *Waynesboro News-Virginian* claimed that "[t]he manner in which he [Harman] met his death was not clear, though one Federal soldier reported him attacked by five men, but he fell in the mud of Main Street at the foot of the hill."[163]

DeWitt Gallaher gave the following account in an earlier newspaper article, which appeared in the *Valley Virginian* on October 15, 1926:

The Cook Building, at present-day 533 Main Street, Waynesboro, Virginia, built circa 1838. This building served as a hospital during the Civil War. George Hawke recounts being told by Curtis Bowman that a Confederate veteran once pointed out damage to the building that had been caused by artillery fire during the Battle of Waynesboro. *Photo by author.*

"Among those mixed up in this terrible retreat was Col. Harman who seeing all was lost, was one of the very last to leave the front line of battle. In the mad rush he was overtaken and shot from his horse in lower Main Street."[164]

In a letter addressed to DeWitt Clinton Gallaher, Samuel V. Woods described what he had witnessed as a young boy from his family's home on Main Street as the battle unfolded. The excerpted letter,[165] which follows, provides an interesting and vivid recounting of that day—including the death of Colonel Harman:

Samuel V. Woods
Lawyer
1008 Kanawha National Bank Bldg.
  Charleston, W. VA   10 Nov. 1926
Dear Mr. Gallaher:

I have read with bated breath and unflagging interest the graphic account you kindly sent me of the battle of Waynesboro of March 2, 1865. From our back porch we watched the fighting on Gallaher's hill and saw the retreat of Confederate men and guns in a precipitate rush down the hill toward [Baylor's] Mill. Where after the battle, we saw the guns spiked and disabled where they had been captured, on the east side of the mill race.

Some of the retreat and fighting was down the Main Street in front of the house, which we witnessed thro [sic] the windows, in spite of the remonstrations of my heroic and devoted mother, alone with a house full of little children, in the midst of the battle, which she knew full well, as many a brave soldier did, that the fight was one of the dying struggles of the prostrate confederacy.

Col. Harman was shot near our house on Main Street, a little beyond and South East of Dr. Alexander's house, whose front porch ran out on the street, the lower, wooden floor of which was nearly on a level with the street, and over this we watched some of the retreating soldiers ride, pressured by the union soldiers, and among them, I think, was Col. Harman, who had been at the Alexander house a moment before. The soldier whose body was found in the mud by the Alexander girls whose body your article states was "<u>carried into a shop</u>" was, I am quite sure, the same confederate soldier who was killed nearly in front of our house, whose body was carried into our vacant store room on the corner opposite Fishburne's house and <u>laid on the counter</u>.[166] I can see his body yet! The events of that fatal day are deeply graven in my mind, never to be erased, tho I was but a small child then. The mud, the mud, the ragged and dirty men, the splashed horses, the firing guns, the boom of cannon, the frightened people, the strange soldiers, the absence of all "our men," the uncertainty of their fate, the alarms of war. How they did affright us!! My father was an assistant quartermaster with, I think, the rank of Captain under Major Henderson M. Bell, himself a lawyer, a law partner of Col. Harman…on the 2 of March 1865 we lived in a brick house on Main Street opposite Fishburnes. What a war it was!! How useless it all seems now! What was settled, which could not have been settled without it?…We surely can see how wisely God overruled it, all for our own good and for the good of our country and the glory of His name.

Other accounts claim that Harman had actually surrendered but was shot anyway. But even General Early wasn't sure about the circumstances surrounding Harman's death, as he revealed in his autobiography after the war:

> *The only person killed on our side, as far as I have ever heard, was Colonel Wm. H. Harman, who had formerly been in the army but then held a civil appointment; and he was shot in the streets of Waynesboro, either after he had been made prisoner, as some said, or while he was attempting to make his escape, after everything was over.*[167]

An article appearing in the *Staunton Republican Vindicator* on March 21, 1865, included the following recounting regarding Harman's death:

> *The precise manner of his death has not been learned…. Shortly after* [the Confederate retreat], *in company with Major Hotchkiss, he stopped at the house of Dr. C. Alexander, where they had been but a short time when they were informed that the enemy were close by. Major Hotchkiss succeeded in mounting his horse before Gen. Harman and the last he saw of Gen. Harman was that he was endeavoring to rally the people and the scattering soldiers in the streets of Waynesboro. A Union officer states that Gen. Harman was ordered to surrender five times and refusing thereby he was fired upon and immediately killed, the ball entering the right side passing through the right lung and penetrating the heart.*

However, the editor of that same paper left no doubt that his opinion was different from what his own paper had reported just three days earlier regarding Harman's death:

> *The editor regrets to announce the death of Colonel William H. Harman, who was trying to rally the troops in Waynesboro on Thursday, March 3, 1865. He was murdered by the enemy after he had surrendered. Although not very old, Harman had already attained a high position in the Virginia Bar, was a Commonwealth's attorney, an officer in the Virginia Regiment in Mexico, a colonel of the 5th Virginia Infantry at the war's beginning, and the commanding officer of the Augusta Reserves. He was a Grand Master of the Grand Lodge of Masons of Virginia, a husband, and a father of six young children.*[168]

Ironically, in that same issue, the paper noted that Harman had read and "forcibly explained…resolutions" to "a large and enthusiastic meeting of the citizens of Augusta County, held at their Court House on Monday the 27th day of February 1865." The first resolution after the preamble was, oddly enough, prophetic for the distinguished Virginian:

Whereas, The people of these Confederate States have had a distinct and unmistakeable [sic] *issue presented to them by the Despotic Ruler of the United States, We are emphatically informed that the abject surrender of our liberty as a people is demanded, and further contumacy and assistance is to be visited with all the horrors of a subjugation which carries in its brain deprivation of personal freedom for ourselves and children; confiscation of our property, and the destruction of every right we hold dear. The Government created by us and fairly representing us, has met this insolent demand with a manly defiance, which we re-echo and endorse. Placing our trust in the Lord of Hosts; relying upon the justice of our cause; preferring death to dishonor— determined to bequeath the precious boon of Independence which we inherited from our Fathers, to our children, or die in the effort; willing to lay our all if need be upon the altar of our country, resolved never to submit to the yoke of such a people as those with whom our brothers and sons have been engaged in deadly struggle for four years, and who have delighted in sacking and destroying our houses, devastating our lands, insulting our women and murdering our citizens; the People of Augusta County have assemble[d] in primary meeting, and do solemnly Resolve:*

1st. That we have a firm and certain conviction of the justice of our cause, and will maintain it at every sacrifice of blood and treasure.

2nd. That the watchfires of Liberty lighted in 1861 burn with undiminished brilliancy in this the 5th year of the cruel war waged against us by our unscrupulous and vindictive foe; and though occasional disasters have and may occur to our gallant armies, they cannot be extinguished until our independence as a people is fully established.

3rd. That the noble, defiant and patriotic resolves coming up daily from our gallant armies in the field and from our people at home, give renewed assurance of unspoken determination to persist in the struggle until that end shall have been attained.

4th. That our subjugation cannot be effected if our people are united—and notwithstanding the vaunted superiority of our enemy in numbers, having full faith in the justice of a righteous God, in the valor of our veteran soldiers and in the patriotism of our people, we may, and do set their threats of extermination at defiance.

5th. That we regard reconstruction as but another name for submission to tyranny, and "we pledge our lives our fortunes and our sacred honor" never to entertain even the idea of it, but to resist it in the future as we have done in the past, to the utmost extremity.

6th. That our confidence in our Rulers, civil and military and our noble armies is unabated.

7th. That for the sustenance and support of our Government and our soldiers we are prepared to meet all demands which are made upon us, and to this end, if it be deemed necessary, we are willing to open our Store Houses, and reduce our families to half rations, or even less.

8th. That having given our sons and brothers to the cause we would be "less than man," if we were not ready to make any sacrifice of property, or hesitate to respond to the calls of our chosen leaders.

9th. That whilst some of our fellow citizens oppose the arming of our negroes, we are content with the knowledge that we have the sanction of God for using all the means in our power to resist wicked oppression, and if this means of resistance be deemed necessary and available by such men as President Davis and by Gen. Robt. E. Lee, we shall not stop to discuss abstract questions, but will cheerfully give our servants, as we have our sons to our country.[169]

Just three days later, Harman lay dead on his hometown's Main Street, having given that ultimate "sacrifice of blood and treasure"—his own life.

It is worth noting that William Harman was a brother to Stonewall Jackson's quartermaster, Major John A. Harman. There were actually five Harman brothers who fought for the Confederacy. Along with William and John, there was also Michael G., Asher W. and Thomas L., who died of typhoid in 1861. The remaining three brothers all survived the war. In a genealogy record published in 1926 and titled *Harman-Garber Record*, the following is noted about these brothers:

At the beginning of the war between the states in April 1861, there lived at Staunton, Virginia, the "Harmans," all natives of Staunton and Augusta County, Virginia. This family consisted of five brothers; Michael G. Harman, John A. Harman, William H. Harman, Asher W. Harman, and Thomas L. Harman. All were in the prime of early manhood, had families and were prominent business men of the town. They were among the first to offer their services to the Confederate cause…. A Yankee officer of distinction who served in the union army who knew these Harman brothers before the war and their war record in the Confederate army said they reminded him of a family of five brothers who served with distinction in the Yankee army and were known as the "Fighting McCooks" and that he thought these Harman brothers should be known in the Confederate army as the "Fighting Harmans."[170]

William Harman was the only confirmed[171] casualty on the Confederate side. There were nine Union soldiers killed.

As Harman lay dying in the street, Early was escaping. Some accounts claim that Early escaped through Rockfish Gap (and that is where the

This is believed to be the approximate location of Colonel William Harman's death, in the street between the three-story building on the corner and the next brick building on present-day Main Street, Waynesboro, Virginia. *Photo by author.*

Federals thought they were pursuing Early), but Early first rode north before heading east across the Blue Ridge Mountains. Early later described his escape as follows:

> [T]*he enemy had got between the mountain and the position where I was, and retreat was thus cut off, I rode aside into the woods, and in that way escaped capture. I went to the top of a hill to reconnoitre, and had the mortification of seeing the greater part of my command being carried off as prisoners, and a force of the enemy moving rapidly towards Rockfish Gap. I then rode with the greater part of my staff and fifteen or twenty others, including General Long, across the mountain, north of the Gap, with the hope of arriving at Greenwood depot, to which the stores had been removed before the enemy reached that place; but on getting near it, about dark, we discovered the enemy in possession. We then rode to Jarman's Gap, about three miles from the depot, and remained there all night, as the night was exceedingly dark and the ice rendered it impossible for us to travel over the rugged roads.* [172]

DeWitt Gallaher provided more detail as to the fleeing Confederates and which mountain gap Early and his staff took to get across the Blue Ridge and elude their pursuers:

> *Wagons, cavalry, hundreds on foot became a mingled mass of crowded fugitives, Yankees on their fleetest horses, trying, as they said, to capture even General Early himself, but he escaped at the ford at the R.R. bridge below and thru Turks Gap six miles away. Nearly every Confederate was captured, and all the artillery, wagons, etc. The prisoners were placed in the meadow at the mill race and sent to Winchester under guard the next day.* [173]

Although Early never specifically mentions Turk Gap, the old road (today a horseback riding trail) descends on the east side of the mountain to a fire road that descends from Jarman Gap. So Gallaher's assertion would make geographical sense when compared to Early's less precise description of his escape route. Even though Early and his staff did not head toward Rockfish Gap, a number of other Confederate soldiers did. Harlan Lloyd described what he witnessed:

> *Captain* [Lycurgus D.] *Lusk and half a dozen men from my own regiment, and as many more from the Eighth New York...dashed along the stony road*

leading up to the gap. The roadway was filled with transportation wagons of Early's command, the ordnance, commissary, and medical supplies having been hastily ordered to Greenwood Station, when Early discovered that Custer's attack was to be a serious one.[174]

Personal anecdotes of battles from soldiers' diaries and memoirs always give color and insight into how men react in life-and-death situations and against one another—particularly one on one and at close quarters. Overall troop movements, positions and strategies of the opposing armies are, of course, necessary to understand how a battle unfolded and why a particular side secured victory. But the personal stories and memories of individual soldiers give us necessary depth and add a human side to these conflicts. A few good examples come to us through the recollections of Sergeant Isaac Cause of Company E, 2nd Ohio Volunteer Company. Sergeant Cause was involved in the movement around Early's left flank. He related the following in his book *Four Years with Five Armies*, published in 1908. As the Confederates ran, not all of them were so anxious to surrender. Cause demonstrated remarkable patience with the uncertain intentions of his enemies:

[T]wo men that had hid in the fence corner rose up and stepped to the middle of the lane. Their looks showed that they had no intention of giving up; but I had the drop on them with my gun over the bars. I demanded their surrender, but they repeatedly made motions to bring their guns into position. They were greeted each time with an injunction not to do it. I also told them to throw down their guns and step ten paces in front of them. They made a move to run, but I insisted that they obey orders, which they finally did. Here I concluded to do something that I had never done before and which I had always discouraged in others whenever talked about. I had recently heard of some depredations of the kind perpetrated by the enemy, and I felt like retaliating. I told them to disgorge, and got one pocketknife, a leather pocket-book with two twenty-dollar Confederate bills, some Southern poetry, and a ring which they said was made of a Yankee's bone.[175]

Cause continued his pursuit of the retreating Rebels and shared this incident, which occurred once he reached the South River:

When I arrived at the bank some were jumping into the river and some were climbing out on the other side. In front of us was a boy about seventeen years old, on an island not much larger than an army wagon, situated in the middle of the river. He was dressed in a new uniform of fine gray cloth and nicely trimmed with black silk braid. When I appeared on the river bank he threw his musket into the water and was about to follow it. A demand not to go caused him to halt, but he continued to assume the posture of one about to plunge, with his weight thrown on his left foot, which was in advance of the right, with arms stretched upwards. Leaning over the water I requested him to return. I made repeated entreaties, and was compelled to threaten to shoot him every time he moved. A half dozen of his comrades stood on the opposite bank watching every motion. He said he had nearly

Bernard Bluecher Graves joined the Hanover Artillery on May 22, 1861. In October 1862, he was transferred to the Amherst Artillery and fought with it for the remainder of the war, a part of the time as a corporal. He was captured near Waynesboro, Virginia, on March 2, 1865, and imprisoned in Fort Delaware. *Courtesy Library of Congress.*

drowned in his effort to get away and would not take the same chance to surrender, but if compelled to take any chances it would be to escape.

While I had no intention of shooting, I was compelled to keep up appearances. Several of the boys had now assembled on the bank, and among them was one mounted man. I asked him if he would come back if we sent him a horse. He said yes. The trooper heard this, and before anyone could speak he plunged into the water, swimming out to him, and the boy got on behind the trooper.[176]

In total, between 1,200 and 1,800 (the exact number is unknown and accounts vary) Confederates were captured, along with all of the Confederates' artillery pieces, numerous wagons and a number of battle flags. Custer reported the following captured:

Among some of the substantial fruits of this victory we had possession of about 1,800 prisoners, 14 pieces of artillery, 17 battle-flags, and a train of nearly 200 wagons and ambulances, including General Early's headquarter's wagon, containing all his official desks and records.[177]

Early scoffed at the numbers claimed by Custer, Sheridan and, later, Ulysses S. Grant:

Grant, in speaking of this affair, says: "He [Sheridan] *entered Staunton on the 2d, the enemy having retreated on Waynesboro—Thence he pushed on to Waynesboro, where he found the enemy in force in an entrenched position, under General Early. Without stopping to make a reconnaissance, an immediate attack was made, the position was carried, and 1,600 prisoners, 11 pieces of artillery, with horses and caissons complete, 200 wagons and teams loaded with subsistence, and 17 battle flags were captured." This is all very brilliant; but unfortunately for its truth, Sheridan was not at Waynesboro, but was at Staunton, where he had stopped with apart of his force; while the affair at Waynesboro was conducted by one of his subordinates. The strength of my force has already been stated, and it was not in an entrenched position. I am not able to say how many prisoners were taken, but I know that they were more than my command numbered, as a very considerable number of recently exchanged and paroled prisoners were at the time in the valley, on leave of absence from General Lee's army. I not only did not have 200 wagons or anything like it, but had no use for them. Where the 17 battle-flags could have been gotten, I cannot imagine.*[178]

The claim for seventeen flags being captured, despite Early's disagreement, comes up in numerous accounts. Historian Jeffry D. Wert related the following about the captured flags in his biography of George Armstrong Custer:

> *As the Federals corralled the captives and vehicles, Captain George B. Sanford of Sheridan's staff rode into Waynesborough and met Custer, who asked if Sheridan was nearby. When Sanford replied that he was en route, Custer reported the number of prisoners, flags, and cannon seized. The aide turned to find Sheridan, to whom he repeated the general's figures. Minutes later, as Sanford recounted it, "up came Custer himself with his following, and in the hands of his orderlies, one to each, were the seventeen flags streaming in the wind. It was a great spectacle and the sort of thing which Custer thoroughly enjoyed."*[179]

The discrepancy between Union claims of eleven artillery pieces captured and Early's (as well as many others') claim that the Confederates had only six pieces of artillery involved in the battle would seem to stem from pieces counted but already in Waynesboro and not part of Early's army or of Nelson's artillery. In explaining his choice of positions, Early would later write, "My object in taking this position was to secure the removal of five pieces of artillery for which there were no horses, and some stores still in Waynesboro…and Nelson had six pieces of artillery."[180]

We also know from various other sources that Nelson had a total of six guns involved in the battle and that those pieces had horses attached to them; Early would also confirm this in his memoirs as he described his army in late 1864: "Nelson's battalion, with some pieces of artillery with their horses, was retained with me, and the remaining officers and men of the other battalions were sent, under the charge of Colonel Carter, to General Lee."[181]

Jedediah Hotchkiss's diary also agrees with Early's accounting: "The enemy left many of the captured wagons and four pieces of artillery, of six they captured, stuck in the mud."[182] And George E. Pond, who was an associate editor of the *Army-Navy Journal*, wrote the following in his book chronicling the final years of the war in the Shenandoah Valley: "[A]nd almost the entire force captured—all Early's wagons and subsistence, tents, ammunition,…eleven guns (including five found in the town)."[183] And General Early provided one more comment that explains the differing accounts regarding the captured artillery pieces: "The greater part of my command was captured, as was also the artillery, which, with five guns on the cars at Greenwood, made eleven pieces."[184]

The Coiner-Quesenbery House, 332 Main Street, Waynesboro, Virginia. This structure, built in 1806, would have witnessed the chaos on the day of the battle. *Photo by author.*

Thus, it can be assumed that Sheridan's army, in capturing Nelson's six guns, as well as the five that were apparently already in Waynesboro with "no horses," simply did not differentiate between the two sets, as they were all Confederate.

Historian Richard L Nicholas wrote that the apparent embellishment of captured inventory "was manifested by the awarding of 15 Medals of Honor for the capture of 14 Confederate flags and the recapture of one Union flag."[185] One of those medal recipients was George Pforr. Pforr was actually a Marylander and Confederate deserter who joined the Union army in February 1864, using the alias Charles W. Anderson. He was awarded the Medal of Honor for the capture of one of the Confederate flags.[186]

Early would later write of his disappointment regarding the "fight"—or lack thereof—that was left in his army that day in March 1865:

> *The only solution of this affair which I can give is, that my men did not fight as I had expected them to do. Had they done so, I am satisfied that the enemy could have been repulsed; and I was and still am of opinion that*

the attack at Waynesboro was a mere demonstration to cover a movement to the south towards Lynchburg. Yet some excuse is to be made for my men, as they knew they were weak and the enemy very strong.[187]

Thus did the War Between the States end in the Shenandoah Valley. In little more than one month, General Lee would surrender to General Grant at Appomattox.

After the battle, an article in the *Republican Vindicator* newspaper of Staunton, dated March 31, 1865, chastised residents of the Valley for not being more supportive of Early's army by supplying food and forage. Although it doesn't tell the whole story (the drought of 1864 and Sheridan's aggressive tactics in both destroying and procuring supplies), it does reveal that there was friction between those who were still holding out hope that the Confederacy could survive and those who were more concerned with their own personal survival over that of the Confederacy's. Regardless, the notion that food and forage alone could have made a difference, as the article suggests, is doubtful given Sheridan's superior numbers and his better-equipped army:

Recent events in our Valley have shown the folly of withholding supplies from our troops. Had Early's army been supported in the Valley, instead of being disbanded for want of food and forage, the recent raid of Sheridan which laid waste the Valley and the Piedmont district could have been checked. Sheridan found the supplies wherever he went, which were withheld from our own soldiers. He reported to his Government that he found food and forage enough in a single county to support his whole army for two months. Had one half of this been furnished to our troops our army would have been retained in an effective condition, and the invaders would have been defeated and our homes saved from desolation.[188]

Although the Battle of Waynesboro appears as inconsequential in many histories of the war, it was not as insignificant as some might believe. Without a clear victory at Waynesboro, Sheridan might not have been able to leave the Shenandoah Valley. And although Early's army was already weakened before the battle, a remnant could still have posed a threat to the Union's need to—once and for all—dominate the Shenandoah Valley and render its usefulness as a food supply for the Confederacy impotent. Custer further noted that the value of the Union victory was "of the highest value and importance to us for another reason; it opened a way across the Blue Ridge Mountains through Rockfish Gap, and thereby saved us from several days'

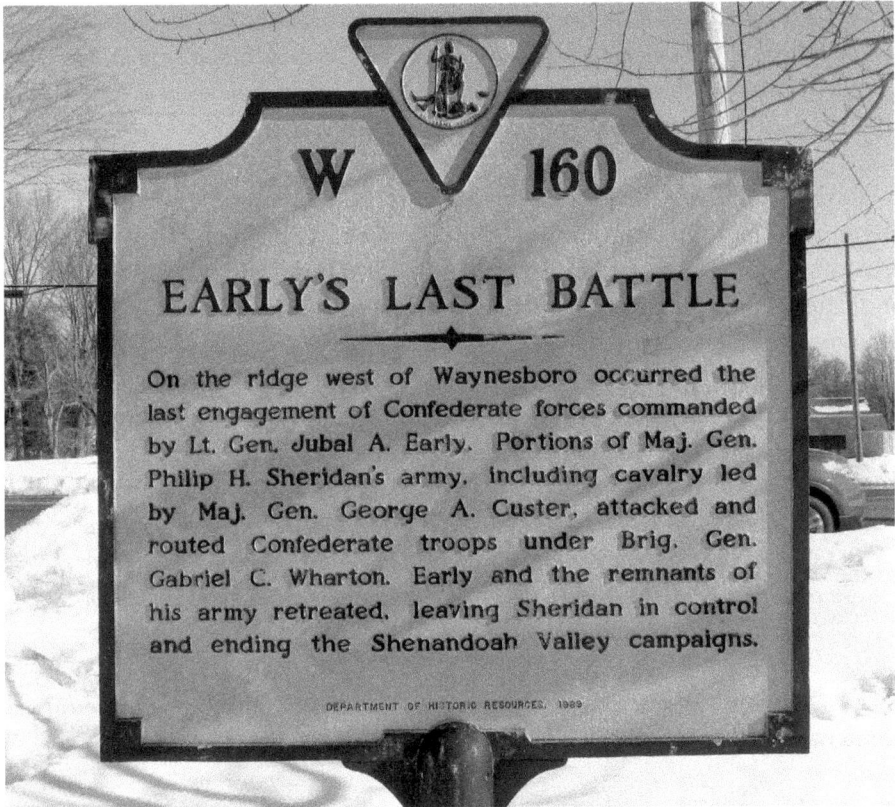

Virginia Historical Highway Marker, Battle of Waynesboro. *Photo by author.*

delay and marching."[189] The Union victory also briefly took the war to areas in Albemarle County and other parts of central Virginia that, up to that point, had not seen a lot of activity. After crossing the Blue Ridge into Albemarle County and Charlottesville, Sheridan's army headed south, destroying the James River Canal locks near Goochland Courthouse. Sheridan would then join the Army of the Potomac near Petersburg on March 26 for the opening of the Appomattox Campaign.

The triumph at Waynesboro was also an important element in strengthening Grant's forces to take Petersburg and eventually bring Lee to terms of surrender at Appomattox. Custer's 3rd Cavalry Division chief of staff, Edward W. Whitaker, expressed the following view about Waynesboro's importance to Union veterans after the war:

The country will never know the whole truth, or how much it owes to General Custer for turning the tide to victory in the last three decisive engagements, Waynesboro, Five Forks and Appomattox Station. Failure in either one of these would have resulted in the prolongation of the war indefinitely.[190]

Early's defeat at the Battle of Waynesboro ultimately resulted in his being relieved of his command. As Early noted in his memoir, he received a communiqué from General Lee dated March 30, 1865. The letter also indicates that, at least publicly, Lee continued to have hopes that his army might prevail. Early noted:

The letter itself, which was written on the very day of the commencement of the attack on General Lee's lines which resulted in the evacuation of Richmond, and just ten days before the surrender of the Army of Northern Virginia, has a historical interest; for it shows that our great commander, even at that late day, was anxiously and earnestly contemplating the continuation of the struggle with unabated vigor, and a full determination to make available every element of success.[191]

Lee's correspondence to Early also reveals his skill in relieving one of his lieutenants in an honorable fashion:

Hd.-Qrs., C.S. Armies,
30th March, 1865.

Lt.-General J.A. Early, Franklin Co., Va.

General,—My telegram will have informed you that I deem a change of Commanders in your Department necessary; but it is due to your zealous and patriotic services that I should explain the reasons that prompted my action. The situation of affairs is such that we can neglect no means calculated to develop the resources we possess to the greatest extent, and make them as efficient as possible. To this end, it is essential that we should have the cheerful and hearty support of the people, and the full confidence of the soldiers, without which our efforts would be embarrassed and our means of resistance weakened. I have reluctantly arrived at the conclusion that you cannot command the united and willing co-operation which is so essential to success. Your reverses in the Valley, of which the public and the army judge chiefly by the results, have, I fear, impaired your influence both with the people and the soldiers, and would add greatly to the difficulties which will, under any circumstances, attend our military operations in S.W. Virginia. While my own confidence in your ability, zeal, and devotion to the cause is unimpaired, I have nevertheless felt that I could not oppose what seems to be the current of opinion, without injustice to your reputation and injury to the service. I therefore felt constrained to endeavor to find a commander who would be more likely to develop the strength and resources of the country, and inspire the soldiers with confidence; and, to accomplish this purpose, I thought it proper to yield my own opinion, and to defer to that of those to whom alone we can look for support.

I am sure that you will understand and appreciate my motives, and no one will be more ready than yourself to acquiesce in any measures which the interests of the country may seem to require, regardless of all personal considerations.

Thanking you for the fidelity and energy with which you have always supported my efforts, and for the courage and devotion you have ever manifested in the service of the country,

I am, very respectfully and truly,
Your ob't serv't,
R.E. LEE, Gen'l.[192]

When the war ended, Early proclaimed, "I cannot live under the same Government with the Yankee" and fled to Mexico. He later went to Canada before finally returning to Virginia in 1869 to again take up his law practice. In 1873, Early founded and became president of the Southern Historical Society. He died in Lynchburg in 1894.

Jubal Early remained an unreconstructed rebel until his death and is considered one of the fathers of the "Lost Cause"[193] tradition. As historian Gary W. Gallagher observed, "Early understood almost immediately after Appomattox that there would be a struggle to control the public memory of the war, worked hard to help shape that memory, and ultimately enjoyed more success than he probably imagined possible."[194] Early's difficulty in accepting the Confederacy's defeat is perhaps best illustrated in the last paragraph of his memoir:

I was not embraced in the terms of General Lee's surrender or that of General Johnston, and, as the order relieving me from command had also relieved me from all embarrassment as to the troops which had been under me, as soon as I was in a condition to travel, I started on horseback to the

Trans-Mississippi Department, to join the army of General Kirby Smith, should it hold out; with the hope of at least meeting an honorable death while fighting under the flag of my country. Before I reached that Department, Smith's army had also been surrendered, and, without giving a parole or incurring any obligation whatever to the Unites States authorities, after a long, weary and dangerous ride from Virginia, through the States of North Carolina, South Carolina, Georgia, Alabama, Mississippi, Arkansas and Texas, I finally succeeded in leaving the country; a voluntary exile rather than submit to the rule of our enemies.[195]

To Early's dying day, he refused to forgive the United States government for crushing the South's war for independence.

Sheridan and Custer would both continue their military careers fighting Indians in the West. And Sheridan would use the methods he had employed in the Shenandoah Valley to subdue Native Americans in the Great Plains: "In an effort to force the Plains people onto reservations, Sheridan used the same tactics he used in the Shenandoah Valley: he attacked several tribes in their winter quarters, and he promoted the widespread slaughter of American bison, their primary source of food."[196]

Sheridan is also remembered for being the driving force behind the creation of Yellowstone National Park. He died of a heart attack on August 5, 1888, and is buried at Arlington National Cemetery. Custer's and Sheridan's paths would cross again, with Sheridan calling his former comrade back into service after Custer was court-martialed in 1867 for being absent from duty during a campaign against the Southern Cheyenne in 1866. Custer, of course, is remembered for his defeat and death at the Little Bighorn on June 25, 1876, at the hands of Arapaho, Cheyenne and Lakota warriors. Remembered in popular memory as "Custer's Last Stand," the epithet and defeat would forever be connected to the commander who routed the Confederates at Waynesboro just eleven years earlier.

After the war, many Waynesboro citizens would have preferred not to remember Sheridan or Custer at all. But they would choose to remember other things and learn to accept the new realities while they planned for the immediate future. One of the structures that witnessed the battle still helps Waynesboro and others remember to this very day.

Chapter 5

AT THE CENTER OF THE STORM

The Plumb House

It…retains much of its integrity.
–National Register of Historic Places Registration Form,
Plumb House

The Plumb House, built between 1802 and 1804, is the oldest frame dwelling located in Waynesboro. Five generations of the Plumb family occupied the home until 1993—likely the longest continuous family-owned and occupied residence in the city. It is located on Main Street, near the center of much of the action that took place between the Confederate and Union armies during the Battle of Waynesboro. After the last member of the Plumb family moved out of the home, the City of Waynesboro purchased the property in 1994. The property is a registered Virginia Historic Landmark, is listed on the National Register of Historic Places and is part of the Virginia Civil War Trails.

In designating the property as worthy to be included on the National Register, the National Park Service noted the following:

The Plumb House is a rare survival: a relatively unaltered circa 1810–20 log dwelling located in a commercial area of Waynesboro, an early Valley of Virginia town that has lost most of its nineteenth-century buildings. The original, main block of the house is a two-story, three bay log structure resting on an uncoursed rubblestone foundation. The house has a central-passage plan created in the mid-nineteenth century

The Plumb House, circa 1870. *Courtesy Waynesboro Heritage Foundation.*

from the original hall-parlor plan. Deeply rooted in the Federal tradition of the Shenandoah Valley...the Plumb House is one of the oldest substantially intact dwellings in the city of Waynesborough, which was laid out in lots in 1797...and incorporated as a town four years later... Architecturally, the house is distinguished by elaborate Federal-style mantels and an exterior chimney of Flemish-bond with patterned glazed headers. Surviving examples of such brickwork are rare in the Valley of Virginia. The property also includes an early smokehouse-cum-summer kitchen...It is a rare survival of an early-nineteenth-century suburban dwelling and retains much of its integrity.[197]

The first member of the Plumb family, Alfred Plumb—whose family had emigrated from Surrey County, England, in 1826—purchased the property from Samuel Brown in 1837 for $600. Plumb died in 1850, and the property was willed to his widow, Mary. She followed her husband in death in 1860. One of Alfred and Mary's sons, Henry, died of wounds received at the battle

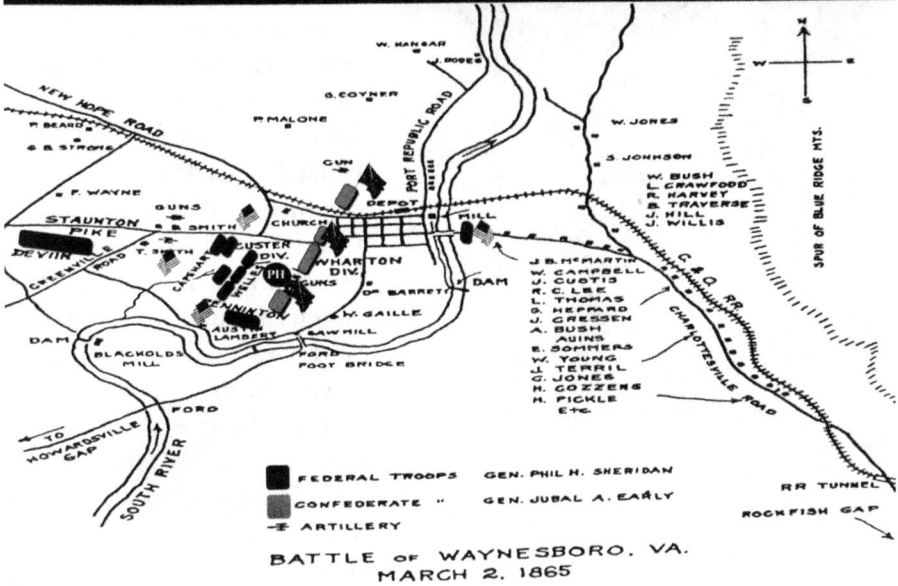

Battle map inside the Plumb House today. *Photo by author.*

of First Manassas. Mary Plumb died without a will, and the eldest son, Alfred Edward Plumb, purchased the property and owned it at the time of the battle. The house is typical of modest structures built in that era—originally constructed of log with clapboard siding added at a later date. The house is two stories and sits on a limestone foundation and cellar. Limestone was used in many early Shenandoah Valley homes due to its abundant availability in the Valley. There are two fireplaces and chimneys in the dwelling. The original property also included other structures common to Shenandoah Valley residents of the nineteenth century: a privy, a slaughterhouse, a combination smokehouse and kitchen and a small barn. Sometime after the original construction and prior to the Civil War, a front porch and interior kitchen were added.

During the battle, the structure suffered some damage to the clapboard siding, and some of it was replaced. Two different types of siding can be seen on the structure today. The original wooden shake roof was removed, and a metal roof was installed after the war.

As the two armies initially faced off at the beginning of the battle, Custer's division was lined up about one hundred yards or so west of the Plumb House,

Musket ball lodged in the Plumb House kitchen door. *Photo by author.*

about where Waynesboro High School stands today. Behind these troops, near the present-day Hardee's restaurant, were artillery commanded by Lieutenant Carle A. Woodruff. Confederate infantry, under the command of Major General Gabriel C. Wharton, were lined up on a ridge that is today Pine Avenue and about one hundred yards east of the Plumb House. In an unpublished essay authored by several descendants of the Plumb family, the following account of the battle's impact on the Plumb House is given:

The Plumb House, 2014. *Photo by author.*

Artillery fuse from the Battle of Waynesboro on display at the Plumb House. *Photo by author.*

The battle began at about 3:00 PM resulting in Federal troops quickly breaking through the Confederate lines and reaching South River. The Plumb House received damage from the east but more so from Union forces to the west. The west chimney was partially destroyed and a cannon ball passed through the chimney, into the living room and cracked the parlor door. The shot shattered a mirror hanging above the mantle in the living room; Union soldiers took the pieces of mirror. A shaving stand said to have been sitting on the mantle has a nick in it reportedly caused by the cannon ball. Other signs of the battle include Happy's discovery of a 2.25 inch diameter, 1.5 pound steel grape shot lodged in the fireplace of the summer kitchen in the 1940s. Also, according to Happy, he related the story told to him that when weather boarding on the house was replaced after the Civil War "a washtub of mini balls was dug from the logs." Musket balls were later found in the wooden shingles under the metal roof when it was replaced in 1983. What appears to be a possible musket ball hole can be seen in the west facing door of the smokehouse. An 1840s vintage Waters flintlock pistol and knife were found in the dirt floor under a meat storage box in the smokehouse when Happy was installing the wooden floor early in 1940. The double edged knife, with a wooden handle, is in excellent condition with little corrosion. The lock of the rusty pistol was never recovered. [198]

Musket ball on display at the Plumb House. *Photo by author.*

Case shot on display at the Plumb House. *Photo by author.*

The Plumb family's oral and written history serves as a wonderful example of how the War Between the States affected families living in its path of destruction and death:

> *Stories about the Civil War were passed down through family members. All of these stories were retold by Miss Willie Ann Plumb…Since Aunt Willie was not born until 1872 she learned them from her mother Mary (Mammy) Plumb but she told them as if she had actually experienced them. Before the battle the Plumbs went to the cellar to escape injury. Aunt Willie's mother wore a new cotton dress which she snagged on a nail. It caused her to remark that "she wouldn't have minded being hurt, but she really hated to see the dress torn." Following the battle, a wounded Union soldier was brought into the house where he was laid on a bed in the second floor front west bedroom. As he lay dying, his friends stayed at the bedside, singing all night. Mary Plumb had baked an "ashcake" (we think) which a Union soldier scooped right out of the skillet; he didn't say a word but left a sack of flour. One day a group of Union soldiers stopped at the house to eat. Mary told them that she would be "feeding Southern soldiers next week" and the officer in charge told her: "Since General Stonewall Jackson was dead, that would not happen." The Union soldier was right. At the Plumb House, Confederate soldiers were fed one day and Federal soldiers the next. Then there was the family story of a "Rebel soldier in the well where he stayed on a rock ledge during the day, coming out at night and hiding in the attic above the main kitchen where he was fed." There was no indication if the soldier was a friend of the family or a relative. The first time Lois went into the kitchen attic many years later she found old tin plates and eating utensils that may have been used by the hidden soldier.*[199]

The Plumb House continued to yield artifacts and stories related to its long history decades after the tumultuous event of the battle. John Plumb shared the following story with me while I was researching this book:

> *In the 1940s, my father was preparing to put a wood floor in the "smokehouse" room of the Summer Kitchen, which is the northeastern room, with the door facing west. The door has a hole in it that may have been a musket ball hole. Daddy moved a wooden meat curing box and stumbled over a pipe sticking out of the dirt. The "pipe" proved to be the muzzle of a flintlock pistol. As the pistol was dug up, he also discovered a knife along with it. The lock to the pistol was not found. It is assumed*

Artifact display at the Plumb House. *Photo by author.*

Wall mural at the Plumb House. *Photo by author.*

Artifact display at the Plumb House. *Photo by author.*

> *that the dirt had not been disturbed since the items were buried; therefore it*
> *is also assumed they were buried during the Civil War. I had someone in*
> *the Auburn University History Department examine the items, and I was*
> *told that the pistol is an 1842 Waters flintlock pistol and the knife is of a*
> *naval design.*[200]

After the City of Waynesboro acquired the property, additional artifacts were discovered.

Today, the dwelling is the home of the Plumb House Museum and is operated by the Waynesboro Heritage Foundation. The museum displays a number of artifacts related to the Battle of Waynesboro as well as other aspects of life in the Shenandoah Valley during the nineteenth century. In addition, there is a collection of birds, butterflies and Native American artifacts on display.

Chapter 6

THE AFTERMATH

Rebuilding and Remembering into a New Century

Now the war is virtually over, and we are—what shall I say?
—Joseph Waddell

The emotions and thoughts that came to Waynesboro residents upon hearing of Lee's surrender and the collapse of the Confederacy ran the gamut of human passions. Former slaves were jubilant and relieved yet were, at the same time, unsure of their future. Among the town's white population, there were feelings of anger and despair, as well as relief and joy. The shock of losing the war left some, as it did historian Joseph Waddell, not knowing what to say. Not surprisingly, bitterness was also a common sentiment among many white citizens of Waynesboro, as it was for other whites throughout the South. That bitterness, and part of the reasons for it, was perhaps best expressed by *Richmond Examiner* newspaper editor E.A. Pollard:

> *The horror and crime of this devastation was remarkable even in Yankee warfare. They impoverished a whole population; they reduced women and children to beggary and starvation; they left the black monuments of Yankee atrocity all the way from the Blue Ridge to the North Mountain. It is remarkable that the worst of Yankee atrocities were always done in the intoxication of unexpected success, when no longer the fears of previous disasters held in check their cruel cowardice, and intimidated their native ferocity.*[201]

Recovery from the brief battle in Waynesboro and, more importantly, the wider devastation to other parts of the Shenandoah Valley would begin immediately with the war's end. But that recovery faced a number of obstacles and would be slow. Fortunes were lost, farms were devastated by Sheridan's Burning and many of the Valley's young, able-bodied men—who would normally be the backbone of an economic recovery—were either dead or wounded. The South's spirit had, in many respects, been broken. Adding to the already difficult circumstances was a three-year drought that followed the end of the war. And just two years after the Valley recovered from the drought came the floods, from rains that began to fall on September 28, 1870. That same evening, Robert E. Lee fell ill up the Valley Pike in Lexington. As Lee lay dying, the rain continued to fall for three days, bringing about one of the worst floods in the history of the Shenandoah Valley. Having just suffered through a devastating war followed by a crippling drought, some Valley residents saw more ominous signs in the torrential rains and flooding. As Lee was breathing his last, historian Douglas Southall Freeman noted that a "flashing aurora lighted the sky for several nights." A Lexington woman opened a copy of *The Lays of the Scottish Cavaliers* and pointed to this passage:

> *All night long the northern streamers*
> *Shot across the trembling sky:*
> *Fearful lights, that never beckon*
> *Save when kings or heroes die.*[202]

The flooding even washed away all the available caskets in Lexington. Local boys found one washed ashore, and although it was actually too short, being undamaged, it was used for General Lee's burial (he was laid to rest without his shoes).[203] At one point, the Shenandoah River was rising at the rate of two feet per hour. The torrent destroyed mills and homes and washed out bridges, roads and telegraph lines—many of which had only been built since the end of the war. There were numerous drownings up and down the Valley. Forty-three died at Harper's Ferry. The South River, which was so important in the building and development of Waynesboro, could also be the source of destruction and ruin. In a *Valley Virginian* newspaper article dated October 6, 1870, the following was noted about some of the damage along the South River:

> *South River—The loss on this river was immense—houses, bridges, fences, corn crops, &c., being swept away by the swollen volume and impetuous*

torrent. Mrs. Kerr, a widow with nine children, lost her dwelling, granary, and orchard. Henry A. Harner lost his chopping mill and saw mill. Wonderlick's saw mill, and the dwelling of his tenant with its contents, in which were included the furniture and clothing of the family, were destroyed. Rippetoe's mill was destroyed. James A Patterson's saw mill was swept away.[204]

Another article in the *Staunton Vindicator* published the following day, while noting the destruction, also revealed the determination of the Valley's hardy citizens:

[S]ome idea may be obtained of the immense destruction which has spread over many portions of our beloved old State, greater, by far, than the devastations of four years [of] war. Our people however, have exhibited in the past a wonderful recuperative power. They will not be downcast now, but will bow with humble resignation to the will of Heaven, and will still hope and strive for the best.[205]

George Hawke wrote of this period in Waynesboro:

It got so bad that at least one local citizen, John B. Smith, resorted to printing his own money. Distilling and undertaking were the businesses to be in. People in unhappy circumstances drink more and die more.[206]

But drinking and dying would not rebuild Waynesboro or the rest of Virginia. The *Staunton Spectator* lectured local citizens on what it was going to take to return to prosperity:

We have already advised, says the Richmond Republic, *all able-bodied men who are not out of employment to go to work on the farm, where there is a great demand for labor. The example set by most of the returned soldiers of General Lee's and Johnston's armies is worthy of general imitation. The large corn crop of the State is due in great measure, to their manly industry. Young men who are lounging about cities and villages in quest of clerkships would do well to imitate the example of the greater number of returned soldiers. They would, besides, secure for themselves much larger pecuniary return than any clerkship, public or commercial, affords. If any of them cherish the delusion that labor is beneath the dignity of a gentleman, we have nothing to say to them. Such hopeless idiots are not to be reasoned with. The time has gone by when labor was the peculiar badge of the servile class. If labor was not respectable formally, it is necessary to make it so now…. Virginia cannot afford now to have a single drone in the hive. The idle man now is the enemy of his State, and ought to be treated as such. Indolence must now be the badge of degradation. Public sentiment should brand with disgrace every creature who, amidst universal poverty, insists upon being consumer and pensions himself upon the public industry. A more disgusting spectacle cannot be found than that of an able-bodied man looking up and down an old family mansion whose inmates are threatened with actual want, whilst broad acres spread around crying out for cultivation, but which he refuses to touch because labor is beneath the dignity of a gentleman. A gentleman indeed! Such an animal has not the faintest conception of what a gentleman means.* [207]

Although the problems and challenges facing the postwar citizens of Waynesboro were formidable, a number of individuals and families in the community rose to the challenge. Newly freed slaves set about establishing their own communities within segregated Virginia. Just east of where Confederate artillerist Private Berkeley had fired his cannon on Sheridan's advancing Yankees, the Port Republic Road neighborhood sprang up, with most of the buildings constructed by Waynesboro's African American residents. Unfortunately, little of anything substantial is known about the Port Republic Road neighborhood regarding the antebellum period. But as was the case in so many black communities after the war, one of the first buildings constructed was a church. Pleasant View Methodist Church was organized in 1867 and constructed its first church building in 1870 on the same site as the present building (312 Port Republic Road). Also forming about the same time was Shiloh Baptist Church. The congregation originally constructed a log structure, which was replaced several years later by a more substantial frame building.

A Virginia Department of Historic Resources study for the neighborhood's historic registration notes the following about the development of the neighborhood:

Port Republic Road's African-American community began to take form after the Civil War. The locale offered a number of attractions to blacks. Port Republic Road adjoined Waynesboro's postbellum industrial section and the tracks and depots of the Chesapeake & Ohio Railroad, which was built between the district and downtown Waynesboro in 1854.

Port Republic Road, Waynesboro, Virginia, circa 1890. *Courtesy Waynesboro Public Library.*

From census schedules it is known that the railroad was a source of employment for Waynesboro blacks during the postbellum period, and presumably the large merchant mill, tanyard and cooper shop located nearby also employed blacks. In the 1880s blacks occupied and owned properties along Arch Street and the 300 block of West Main Street in the downtown, areas located immediately across the railroad tracks from the Port Republic Road neighborhood, which therefore may be considered an extension of the downtown black community. (No above-ground resources associated with the in-town black community apparently survive.) Underlying these local factors in the community's development is the deeper one of the profound social and economic changes that resulted from the Civil War. [208]

By 1885, the community had land donated by local citizens Joshua and Nancy Hill "for use as a colored cemetery for the burial of colored persons." This became Fairview Cemetery and is still in use today. Education was, of course, extremely important to black residents who suddenly found themselves free a little more than a month after the Battle of Waynesboro. At least one black schoolhouse had been built in Waynesboro by 1871. By the early twentieth century, a school that stood at the north end of the neighborhood "contained two rooms, and students were taught only through the seventh grade."[209] But the members of the community sought better educational opportunities for their children:

> *In the 1910s Waynesboro's African American community began to push for improved school facilities. A Parent's League was formed to raise funds and additional monies were donated by the Rosenwald Fund, a philanthropic organization headed by Sears Roebuck executive Julius Rosenwald that assisted the construction of black elementary high schools throughout the South. A new facility known as…Rosenwald School was erected in 1924…The original building and a 1934 addition were replaced by the present facility in 1959, but a 1938–39 auditorium/gymnasium and a 1951 addition were retained.*[210]

Along with the growing religious and educational opportunities came commercial activity. A business directory published in 1893 indicates that there were at least two black businessmen in Waynesboro at the time: a "tobacconist" named Robert Cousins and a barber by the name of D.T. Young. By the mid-1920s, economic development had progressed significantly:

> *A 1926 tax rate directory lists a broom factory, two restaurants, a barber shop and beauty parlor, a dance hall, a pool room, and a general store…. An important addition was made to the neighborhood's commercial component in 1940 with the construction of the…Tarry's Hotel, which replaced a shoe shop and one or more restaurants at the same location… several physicians also maintained offices.*[211]

This commercial activity provided some job opportunities for neighborhood residents, although most held jobs outside the tight-knit community in Waynesboro and surrounding Augusta County. The neighborhood continued to grow and exist as a thriving, independent community through the first half of the twentieth century. In addition to Tarry's Hotel, a 1951 city directory listed "the Casa Blanca Restaurant, the Dew Drop Inn, the Ideal Barber Shop, the Harry Brown and Monroe pool halls, the Methodist and Baptist Churches, and Rosenwald School." A longtime resident of the community, Mrs. Lillian Clark, wrote a wonderful—almost idyllic—description of what life was like within the vibrant Port Republic Road neighborhood during the first half of the twentieth century:

William H. Johnson and his horse, Nellie, circa 1925. Johnson, who was a resident of Waynesboro and was born in 1847, worked for a feed company and coal yard on Ohio Street, near the Port Republic neighborhood. His salary was three dollars per week. Johnson lived to be ninety-four years of age. *Courtesy Waynesboro Heritage Foundation.*

Port Republic Road and adjoining streets formed a unified black community. Except leaving home for daily employment in the city of Waynesboro, everyone was content to always return to their families and friends. Walking through the neighborhood, greetings were exchanged with teachers, ministers, doctors, and business owners…. A pool room once stood on the corner of what is now Port Republic Road and Minden Place. A spring flowed in the lot across the street. Children from the neighborhood played baseball on the lot during the summer. The long hill was excellent for sleigh rides in the winter. Walking through the alleys during the summer, vegetable gardens, chicken yards, cows and pigs could be seen at most homes. City ordinances did not prohibit livestock in those days. With little extra money to spend, families found it economical to be as self-sufficient as possible. Not having a vegetable garden and livestock was considered lazy and poor management by most of the black citizens.[212]

Despite the injustices of the segregationist era, pride in community and a "sense of place" was evident among the inhabitants of the Port Republic neighborhood. Unfortunately, decline came to the community in the second half of the twentieth century, with most businesses closing or moving. Today, the neighborhood exists principally as a residential area, although the former Rosenwald School building still stands and has been converted into a community center. In 2002, the neighborhood was listed on the National Register of Historic Places.

The postbellum period in Waynesboro produced a number of notable African American citizens. One such person was Reverend William Henry Sheppard, who was born in Waynesboro just six days after the battle, on March 8, 1865. Sheppard was the son of free blacks. His father was a sexton in the local Presbyterian church, and Reverend Sheppard's biographer, William E. Phipps (also a native of Waynesboro), believes that William Sr. was likely one of the local black residents pressed into service by the Union army in September 1864 to destroy railroad tracks near Waynesboro.[213] Phipps described the Sheppard family environment:

> *William Sheppard, Sr. was the village barber and the sexton for the brick Presbyterian Church. The Sheppard family were devout members of that church, the oldest one in the community. His wife expressed her faith by praying with her son as well as by her generosity. Her son later gave this tribute: "Mother never turned anyone from her door who came begging, whether white or colored, without offering them such as she had."*[214]

The Sheppard family was as close to being middle class as most black residents could have hoped for, given the realities of the times. And they apparently enjoyed amicable relationships with Waynesboro's white population—a fact Sheppard alludes to in his brief autobiography: "The white people were always very kind to us—as they were to all the colored people."[215] Part of that impression was evidently made on young William by two white women in the community. Sheppard would later write:

> *My first impression on the subject of being a missionary—while still a barefoot boy a beautiful Christian lady, Mrs. Ann Bruce, said to me one day, "William, I pray for you, and hope some day you may go to Africa as a missionary." I had never heard of Africa, and those words made a lasting impression. God bless that good lady, so interested in me and Africa.*[216]

William Phipps related the following story about Sheppard's relationship with some of Waynesboro's white population, including Miss Lou Withrow (the same woman who had so much "stick-to-it-ive" in her nature that she refused to dismiss her school class during the Battle of Waynesboro until she had heard the "roar of the cannon"). This incident illustrates that while Sheppard was treated with a certain amount of respect, he was still not considered an equal among whites:

> *My mother told me of a time when Sheppard returned to his childhood church where she was a member.... After leaving the church he was invited by Lou Withrow, who had first encouraged him to become educated, to her home for dinner. She lived in one of the oldest and finest houses in Waynesboro. Those who gathered there wanted to ask him questions, but it was taboo for blacks and whites to sit around the same table. A window separating the dining room from the back porch provided a creative solution to the problem. On the porch a small table was set for Sheppard next to the raised window, and all sat around what appeared to be an extended table. Conversation, along with the food, then passed back and forth between Sheppard and members of one of his supporting congregations.*[217]

William Sheppard on the mission field in Africa with some Baketti warriors, circa 1900.
Courtesy Presbyterian Historical Society, Presbyterian Church, Philadelphia, Pennsylvania.

William Sheppard attended the Hampton Institute in Hampton, Virginia, where one of his instructors was Booker T. Washington. Sheppard would go on to study at Tuscaloosa Theological Institute, now Stillman College. Stillman's library is dedicated to Sheppard. He would be ordained to the ministry in 1888. After a few brief pastorates in the South, Sheppard went to Africa as a missionary. His first two children would die there. He eventually returned to the United States and pastored a church in Louisville, Kentucky. He died there in 1927.

Other African Americans would make their mark on postwar Waynesboro as well—as educators, ministers, business owners and

Reverend Nelson Durrett. *Courtesy Waynesboro Heritage Foundation.*

REV. NELSON DURRETT

GOD'S DEALER

He has been in preaching since 16 years old.

SERVICE FREE

I preach free to white and colored.

BORN IN NELSON COUNTY

AGE 86   28 OF APRIL

ANY DONATION IS APPRECIATED

Reverend Nelson Durrett's calling card. *Courtesy Waynesboro Heritage Foundation.*

craftsmen. Another African American minister who was born before the Civil War and became well known after the war was Reverend Nelson Durrett. An article that appeared in a July 1975 issue of the *Waynesboro News-Virginian* notes that Durrett could often be seen walking along the streets of Waynesboro preaching the gospel to anyone who would listen. He had a unique way of calling attention to his message, as noted by the newspaper article: "His trademark, as he moved along the streets of the city was a bugle, which he would blow with gusto as an attention-getter." A business card described his ministry:

> REV. NELSON DURRETT
> GOD'S DEALER
> He has been in preaching since 16 years old.
> SERVICE FREE
> I preach free to white and colored.
> Born in Nelson County
> Age 86
> ANY DONATION IS APPRECIATED

The article also noted that to supplement donations, Durrett "often sold chinkapins [*sic*], sassafras roots, huckleberries and other delicacies native to our area."[218]

While preaching on the streets of Waynesboro, Reverend Durrett may very well have encountered and conversed with my great-grandfather Charles Lockridge McGann. Both men shared a common Christian faith, and both were originally from Nelson County, across the Blue Ridge from Waynesboro. McGann's obituary, appearing in the *Waynesboro News-Virginian* in March 1953, gives some background and insight into what life was like after the war for some Waynesboro citizens:

Charles L. McGann

Waynesboro, March 4 [1953]—Charles Lockridge McGann, 82, a resident of Waynesboro for 52 years, died at 4:10 am today at his home, 577 Locust Ave., after a long illness.

Mr. McGann was a familiar figure on Waynesboro streets, taking a daily walk downtown from his home. He retired from active farming and caretaking about four years ago, but continued to work around his home in the yard and garden. He was a lifelong member of the Main Street United Methodist Church and was a member of the church's Baraca Class when it was formed in 1913. He was treasurer of the group for 35 years.

Mr. McGann was born June 22, 1870, in Nelson County, son of the late J.W. McGann. He and his family moved to Waynesboro 52 years ago from their home in Nelson County.

Mr. McGann is survived by his wife, Mrs. Georgie Campbell McGann; one son, Gordon (Mac) McGann, Waynesboro; three daughters, Mrs. Fred Busic and Mrs. J. Frank Mahler, both of Waynesboro, and Mrs. R.M. Vance, Fishersville; one brother, C.H. McGann, Iron Gate; two sisters, Mrs. Brent Lowe, Iron Gate and Mrs. L.J. Dameron, Knoxville, Tenn., three grandchildren and seven great-grandchildren.

The body will remain at the Etter Funeral Home. Funeral Services will be held at 10 a.m. Friday in the Chapel of Etter Funeral Home, conducted by the Rev. John R. Hendricks. Interment will be in Riverview Cemetery. Active pallbearers will be: C.M. Kefauver, Homer Luthers, J.E. Kiger, R.H. Clemmer, S.C. Leavell, and T.W. Shiflet. Honorary pallbearers will include members of the Baraca Class of the Main Street United Methodist Church.

The son of a Confederate soldier, Charles (or "Mr. Charlie," as he was known around Waynesboro) McGann is, in many ways, representative of some of the lower and lower middle-class whites who, like ex-slaves, helped rebuild towns across the South after the Civil War. He and his family would slowly eke out a living by working for families who, despite the economic devastation the Civil War brought to the South, managed to hang on to more resources and begin rebuilding their lives and fortunes. One of the pallbearers listed in McGann's obituary—R.H. Clemmer—is illustrative of those relationships. Much of what I know of that relationship comes through my family's oral history, related to me by my father and grandmother. "Captain Dick" Clemmer was a retired World War I army captain who would be largely responsible for building what would eventually come to be known as Virginia Metalcrafters. As VM's website notes:

> *Virginia Metalcrafters was founded on October 6ᵗʰ, 1890, as the W.J. Loth Stove Company. Located in Waynesboro, Virginia, on the western slopes of the Blue Ridge Mountains in the beautiful Shenandoah Valley, the company manufactured cast iron stoves and wood and coal heaters. The company's motto at the time was, "Loth Stoves Make Happy Homes."*
>
> *Loth, together with his son Percy, made the decision in the late 1890s to add frying pans, waffle irons, tea kettles and other cookware to the company's product line. Some of the tools used to make those original cooking products are still in the company's archives.*[219]

Loth was born in Richmond in 1844 and joined the Confederate army in 1861 at the age of seventeen. He was soon captured and remained a prisoner for the duration of the war. Working in a Richmond stove factory after the war, Loth acquired the knowledge necessary to begin his own stove company after moving to Waynesboro in 1890 and building a factory on the banks of the South River. Loth died in 1904, and his son, Percy, ran the company with the help of his cousin, Richard Clemmer. In the 1920s, the W.J. Loth Company invented and patented a revolutionary electric stove that came to be known as "Hotpoint." General Electric bought the patent in 1930. Despite a temporary closing, the company managed to weather the Depression through a merger with Rife Ram Works. My grandmother Helena McGann Williams would be one of two women employed there by 1937. In 1938, Clemmer made a decision that would allow the company to grow and prosper through the 1990s. The company's website explains:

> *In 1938, the company installed equipment for melting brass and other non-ferrous metals and began to market products under the name Virginia Metalcrafters.*

Although World War II halted the casting of brass products, immediately after the war, Clemmer continued developing the gift line. In 1946 he met and retained the services of artist Calvin Roy Kinstler and commissioned him to do a carving of the great horse Citation. Kinstler completed his work in 1949, shortly after Citation had won the Triple Crown.... Similarly, Clemmer worked with an internationally known sculptor, Oskar Hansen, whose works included the huge angels seen today at either end of the Hoover Dam. Hansen settled in Nelson County, just east of the Blue Ridge Mountains and carved many patterns for Captain Dick, among them, dozens of leaf shapes. Modeled directly from nature, these leaves range in size from 3 inches to 40 inches and many were actively sold until 2005.

Continuing the development of the gift line, Clemmer signed a license with Colonial Williamsburg in 1951 to produce brass and iron reproductions. The company's hand casting and finishing methods were the same as those used to form the original antiques. Williamsburg was just the first of many museum licenses. Virginia Metalcrafters manufactured licensed products

Brass Confederate Campaign Hat paperweight, manufactured by Virginia Metalcrafters. *Photo by author.*

Great Seal of the Confederacy trivet, manufactured by Virginia Metalcrafters. *Photo by author.*

for Colonial Williamsburg, The Smithsonian Institution, Mount Vernon, Monticello, Historic Charleston, Winterthur, Historic Newport, Old Salem, Old Sturbridge Village and The National Trust for Historic Preservation.

Virginia Metalcrafters also manufactured at least two Civil War brass pieces: a Confederate "Campaign Hat" and a "Great Seal of the Confederacy" trivet. After closing in 2005, Colonial Williamsburg bought a number of the Virginia Metalcrafters' molds and still uses them to this day to produce the same quality items formerly produced and sold by VM.

The relationship that my great-grandfather (and later my grandmother) had with Captain Clemmer also extended to that of being neighbors. Clemmer would come to own and develop the area that was known as Gallaher's Woods—the area on which some of the Battle of Waynesboro took place. He developed that into an upscale neighborhood of homes known as Forest Hill. Clemmer himself built a sprawling, Tudor Revival–style house there in 1927 on Locust

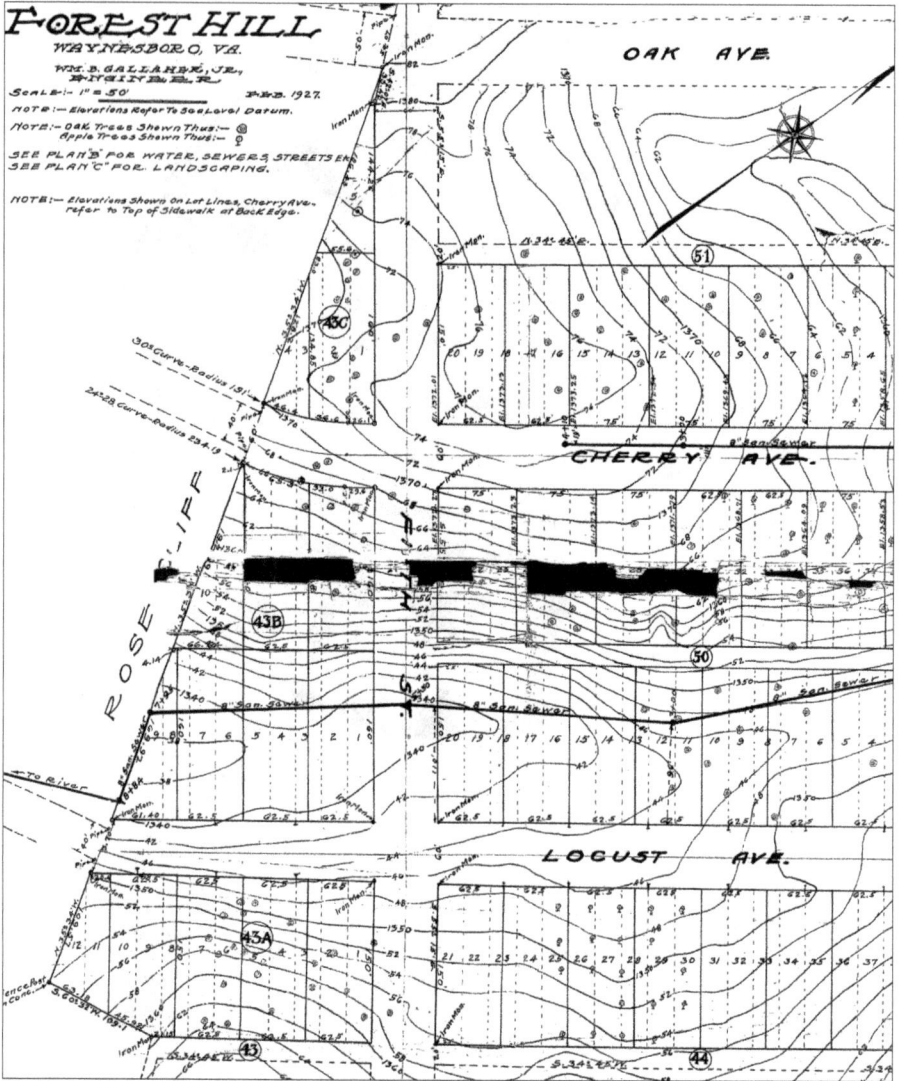

A 1927 survey of a portion of the former Waynesboro battlefield, developed into Forest Hill. Note that the survey work was completed by William B. Gallaher Jr., whose family once owned the property and whose father served in the Confederate army. *Author's collection.*

Avenue. Although my grandparents' (and great-grandparents') home was not part of that neighborhood, their home was separated by only one street, and they became friends and neighbors of the Clemmers. According to my family's oral history, Charles McGann plied his "caretaking" skills in helping tend to the Clemmers' extensive gardens and landscaping. A 2002 National Register of

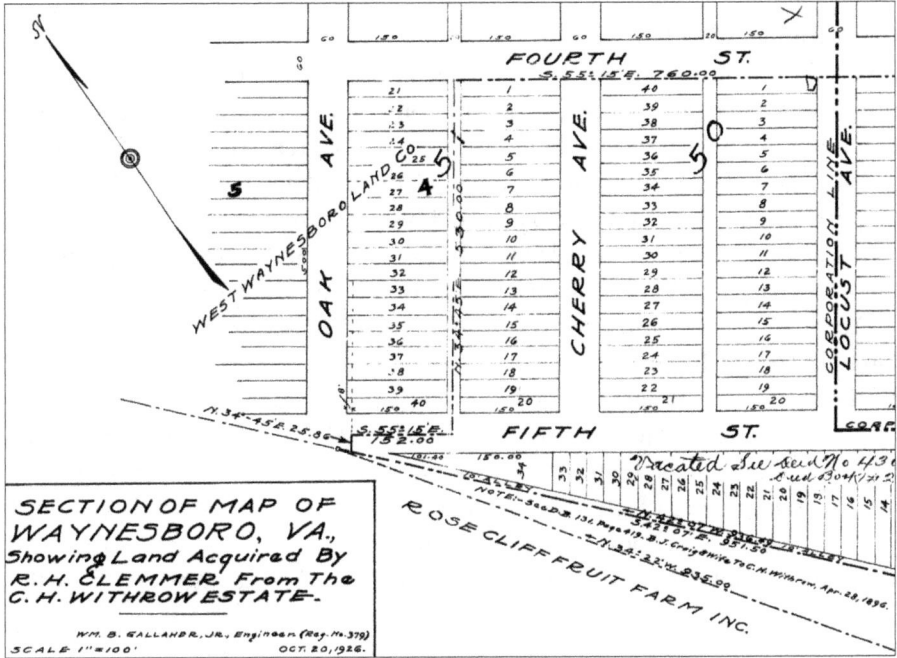

Another survey of portions of the Waynesboro battlefield by William B. Gallaher Jr., 1926. *Author's collection.*

Historic Places registration form for the Tree Streets neighborhood notes the following about the house and gardens:

> *Their 1927 house, designed by a California architect, was the first in the Forest Hills section, which the Clemmers developed. The rock came from Afton Mountain near Swannanoa, and landscape architect A.A. Farnham designed the gardens, which took forty-five years to perfect according to his plans...[the] multi-level pleasure garden...[was] implemented in stages by the Clemmer family over several decades. The large, steeply sloped lot incorporates numerous terraces defined by rock retaining walls and staircases, a shallow pond, a paved patio and grill area, and numerous cutting gardens with choice peonies, roses, and other heirloom and ornamental plantings. Numerous mature trees dot the parcel, and a tall perimeter hedge of American boxwood shelters the entire grounds from the adjoining streets.*

As a child, I was always warned by my grandmother to "stay out of Mrs. Clemmer's gardens!" But it was an enchanting place of solitude and beauty that I frequented often, as had my father growing up on Locust Avenue—no doubt tagging along with "Mr. Charlie" as he performed his caretaking duties. I even recall family members (long since deceased) discussing the fact that Clemmer had something to do with my great-grandfather building a home on Locust, although I don't recall the details. Captain Clemmer acquired much of the former battlefield property in the mid-1920s from the estate of another prominent Waynesboro family and person with whom my great-grandfather enjoyed friendship, as well as employment.

According to an obituary appearing in the *Confederate Veteran*, "Colonel"[220] Charles Howard Withrow was born in Waynesboro on February 6, 1838. Withrow's father, William, served as mayor and owned a large brick home on the south side of Main Street, next to Bruce's Alley. The elder Withrow also served a term as the town's mayor. The family was active in community affairs as members of the Presbyterian church and also as early pioneers in Waynesboro's schools, including what would become, after the war, Fishburne Military School. The home on Main Street also served as the

Withrow home, Main Street, Waynesboro, Virginia, circa 1860. *Courtesy Waynesboro Heritage Foundation.*

town's post office and a store. The obituary notes that Withrow attended private schools as a boy in Waynesboro and earned an MA degree from the University of Virginia in 1860. He taught briefly in Natchez, Mississippi, but joined the Richmond Howitzers upon the outbreak of the Civil War. Withrow was initially commissioned as a lieutenant and was attached to a corps of civil engineers. He later joined Major General Thomas Lafayette Rosser's staff in January 1865 and was promoted to captain.

Records are not clear as to whether Withrow was actually present at the Battle of Waynesboro as part of Rosser's staff. According to oral family history shared with me by a descendant of the Withrow family, Mary Highsmith, Withrow was presented with a sword after the war that the giver claimed was present at the Battle of Waynesboro. This could indicate that it was given in connection to Withrow's connections to Waynesboro, the war, the battle or all three, but that is conjecture. After the war, Withrow returned to teaching, filling "the chair of Greek at Hampden-Sidney College and afterwards taught in Kentucky." He married Mary Shyock in 1874, and their union produced two sons, both of whom died in infancy. Grieving would not soon end for Charles Withrow, as his wife died in 1878. He would never remarry. After his wife's death, Withrow moved to Augusta, Georgia. There he became a member of the faculty for the Richmond County Military Academy, also referred to as the Richmond Academy and the Academy of Richmond County. The school dates to 1783. He would also serve as the school's principal there for twenty-nine years. While at Richmond Academy, Withrow had the reputation of a "disciplinarian" and "was singled out for mention in his first year on the Academy faculty for 'the superior order which had prevailed in the main recitation hall...of which he was in charge.'"[221]

Colonel Charles H. Withrow. *Author's collection.*

A Union cavalry sword presented to Colonel C.H. Withrow. Withrow family oral history asserts that the sword was taken at the Battle of Cold Harbor and was carried at the Battle of Waynesboro. *Photo by author.*

Upon leaving Richmond Academy, Withrow returned to his hometown of Waynesboro, where he taught at Fishburne Military School and was twice elected as the town's mayor between the years of 1914 and 1918. The obituary notes that Withrow was "well-beloved by the people of that community and appreciated for his many virtues" and also that he "was a man of brilliant intellect and broad culture and was considered one of the foremost educators of his time, leaving the imprint of his genius upon the records of his labors and achievements."[222]

Another copy of an obituary in my files that appeared in the *Augusta (GA) Chronicle* (date unknown) gives even more detail about the life of Withrow and the impact he had on those he knew:

Col. Chas. H. Withrow

The announcement of the death of Colonel Charles H. Withrow, which is carried in the local columns of the paper today will be the occasion of widespread regret throughout this community, where he was so well known and so highly esteemed. Many of the most successful business and professional men of middle age in the city today were former pupils of Colonel Withrow, not only at the Richmond Academy, but at his summer home in Waynesboro here, where he taught a summer class for a number of years.

He was a man of most unusual and striking personality; a man whose keenness of intellect was equaled by a physical strength of vigor that made him, after he was long past middle life, possess a vitality and a gift for getting all possible healthy enjoyment out of life, that many young men of twenty might envy. He was a man of clean life, of high thoughts, of broad culture, and one whose word was ever as sacred as his bond.

One of the most striking traits of Colonel Withrow was his marvelous memory. He never forgot a date or a historical fact, and his tenacious memory, coupled with his omnivorous reading, made him one of the best informed men in the entire country. While sometimes seemingly stern to the boys he taught, they all learned to respect and like him, for they knew they would always receive fair treatment at his hands, and that under a surface of sternness beat the kindest heart in the world.

He was a man of most intense loyalty, and his devotion to the Lost Cause of the Confederacy was evidenced by the fact that he never missed a chance to get with his Veteran friends, and, long after he left Augusta [Georgia], he always joined camp 435 at the annual reunion, and marched with them in the familiar gray uniform. The last time he marched with the camp was at the reunion in Atlanta two years ago.

A loyal Southerner, a cultured scholar, a faithful friend, one who lived up to every obligation that life imposed upon him, and that made life pleasant for those about him—has gone. He was the highest and best type of the gentleman of the old South, and as long as any that knew him are living in Augusta the memory of "the Colonel" will live in the hearts of his friends here.[223]

In an article published in the *Waynesboro News-Virginian* on November 14, 1992, local historian Curtis Bowman gave details surrounding Withrow's last day in this world and the legacy that he left to Waynesboro:

Col. Withrow remained in good health until the day of his death. He had made the usual two or three walks from his home to and from Fishburne's corner during the day, and the family was making preparations for celebrating his approaching 83rd birthday in a couple of weeks.

About ten o'clock at night he complained of chest pains, and the family immediately sent for Dr. Richardson, who lived just around the corner across from the newly completed post office on Wayne Avenue. Dr. Richardson responded immediately and diagnosed an acute heart problem; despite the doctor's best efforts, Col. Withrow died about two hours later.[224]

The article goes on to discuss Withrow's funeral, noting that "the entire Fishburne Military School Cadet Corps attended as Escort of Honor." At a special meeting of the town council the following week, "resolutions were passed commemorating Col. Withrow's long and fruitful service," citing him as "a gallant Confederate veteran, brilliant scholar, eminent educator and loyal citizen."

The *Confederate Veteran* obituary states that after Withrow retired permanently, he "devoted his time to his farming and fruit-growing

Charles H. Withrow headstone, Riverview Cemetery, Waynesboro, Virginia. *Photo by author.*

interests." And although it notes that Withrow died "in the home where he died" (on Main Street), his family also owned a home on Pine Avenue, just two city blocks from my grandparents' home on Locust. Colonel Withrow also owned a significant amount of acreage surrounding this home where he farmed and maintained his orchard, consisting primarily of apple trees. It is Withrow's "farming and fruit-growing interests" that was at least in part responsible for the close relationship that would ultimately develop between Withrow and my great-grandfather Charles McGann. According to descendant Mary Highsmith, the home on Pine Avenue was actually built (or purchased) by the Withrow family "to accommodate Withrow children members who came back to Waynesboro to live following the untimely death of their mother."

The 2002 Tree Street National Register of Historic Places registration form notes the following about the home:

> *Two-story Queen Anne house of stuccoed frame construction with a metal-sheathed gable roof. The house has front and side two-story bay windows with usual hip-and-gable roofs and louvered gable vents of unusual Tudor-arched shape. The one-story front porch has slender classical columns and a smaller second-story sleeping porch. Other features include a brick foundation, a two-tier side porch with modern wood exterior stair, two two-*

*tier rear porches (one enclosed, the other with matchboard railings), and
2/2 windows. The house may be that owned by Louisa Withrow in 1892
and it may be portrayed in the 1891 aerial perspective of Waynesboro.
The hip-and-gable form of its bay window roofs suggests and [sic]
affinity with the contemporaneous Queen Anne houses at 428 Maple and
517 Walnut. It was listed as the Belgravia Apartments in 1935, and it
appears to have been remodeled during the early twentieth century, perhaps
during its conversion into apartments. (Tax records; Hawke,* History of
Waynesboro, *front end sheets.)*[225]

Local historian Curtis Bowman claimed in his *Waynesboro Days of Yore*
(volume 1) book that the house was built by Charles Withrow.[226] That claim
is questionable, as Withrow did not live in Waynesboro at the time. My
father related to me that his grandfather Charles McGann told of caring
for the Confederate veteran's old horse, Bird. Bowman shed additional
light on that relationship, as well as other activities at the Withrow home
on Pine Avenue:

*A Mr. Thompson and family rented the property...There were three
beautiful Thompson daughters; Hood, Champe and Louise. Until they
were married, the home was a beehive of activity. We often sat on our porch*

Withrow family portrait, circa 1902. Colonel Withrow is standing, center, second row. Lou
Withrow is seated, second from left. *Courtesy Waynesboro Heritage Foundation.*

Withrow home on Pine Avenue, Waynesboro, Virginia. *Photo by author.*

and watched the "comings and goings" of the girls and their beaux up the street…. Col. Withrow would often ride up to the Thompson house astride his sleek black horse "Bird." Although there was a stepping stone and hitching post, he never dismounted, but sat flicking his riding crop against the shiny surface of his boot while he waited for the occupants to come out to talk…. Mr. Charles McGann lived at the corner of Fourth (Fourteenth) St. and what is now Locust. He farmed some, and had a barn for "Bird" and a pair of draft horses. The barn was later converted into a dwelling.[227]

Upon reading that information (originally published as an article in the *Waynesboro News-Virginian*), my father wrote to Bowman about his memories of his grandfather "Mr. Charlie" and the feeding of the Colonel's horse:

I was raised in the house which you reference as being located on the corner of Fourth (Fourteenth) Street, and I currently own this property. As a small boy, I frequently accompanied "Mr. Charlie" on his visits to the barn to feed the black horse "Bird."[228]

U.S. cavalry horse bit that once belonged to Colonel Withrow. *Photo by author.*

Presentation cups that once belonged to Colonel Withrow. *Photo by author.*

My father went on to describe an old photograph of Withrow, two silver-plated pewter cups and a Federal cavalry horse bit, all given to his grandfather—and then passed to him—by Colonel Withrow. One of the pewter cups is inscribed, "Col. C.H. Withrow from Class of '91." The other is inscribed, "From Class of '08 A.R.C." The "A.R.C." is for Academy of

Richmond County, from which Withrow retired in 1907. That same year, my great-grandfather purchased four lots "near the corporate limits of the town of Waynesboro, Virginia," and two years later, in 1909, he began building his home on Locust Avenue. One of the building material invoices for that home, dated February 25, 1909, was paid, in part, from a check issued by "C.H. Withrow" in the amount of $12.50.

Further evidence of the closeness of my great-grandfather to the Withrow family is illustrated by the names he gave his own children. Charles Withrow had a sister with the first name of Helena, a nephew with the first name of Gordon, a niece with the first name of Nettie and a sister named (after marriage) Bettie Withrow Chase. My great-grandfather named three of his children Helena Chase (my grandmother), Gordon and Nettie. According to Mary Highsmith, Colonel Withrow's "nephews & nieces were very important to him because his own children had died as babies and he didn't really get to have relationships with them."

Fiftieth-anniversary reunion Company E, 1st Virginia Cavalry, April 19, 1911, at the Brunswick Hotel on South Wayne Avenue, Waynesboro, Virginia. *Courtesy Waynesboro Heritage Foundation.*

Of course, there were other Civil War veterans who returned and contributed to both the rebuilding and remembering after the war. On April 19, 1911, remnants of the Valley Rangers, Company E, 1st Virginia Cavalry, gathered in Waynesboro to commemorate the fiftieth anniversary of their leaving Waynesboro on their march to Harper's Ferry. This reality of having to simultaneously rebuild and remember was best expressed in the words of the keynote speaker, H.H. Kerr:

> *The Confederate Soldier stepped from the trenches into the furrow. He abandoned the rebel yell to enter the forum, he gave up the sword to enter the battles of commerce and finance, and in a few, short, swift years this land of desolation and death blossomed forth in plenteousness and beauty, leaving only graves, monuments, precious memories and veterans to tell the tale of that awful struggle.* [229]

RE-UNION

Co. E, 1st. Va. Cavalry

Waynesboro, Virginia

April 19, 1911

Cover of printed commemorative program for Company E, 1st Virginia Cavalry, Waynesboro, Virginia, April 19, 1911. *Courtesy Library of Virginia.*

Sergeant Elliott Guthrie Fishburne, who wrote the eloquent recounting of the Valley Rangers marching off to war from Waynesboro, returned to the Valley after the war and went back to his business as a merchant. First operating a store in Millboro Springs called "Fishburne's Cheap Cash and Trade Store," he ultimately returned to the original location on Main Street in downtown Waynesboro. Upon entering into a partnership with a local physician, Dr. J.S. Myers, the general merchandise store became primarily a drugstore, operating on the corner of Main Street and Wayne Avenue. Later on, a soda fountain bar, a jukebox, booths and stools would become

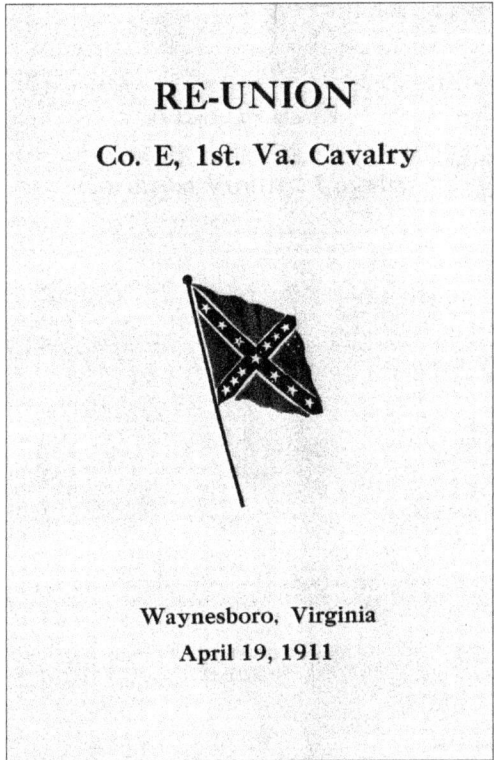

part of the thriving store as well. In 1898, a registered pharmacist joined the business. From the 1890s through 1979, when the building was torn down, Fishburne Drug Store was a familiar landmark in downtown Waynesboro. Generations of merchants, businessmen, Fishburne cadets and teenagers made it a social gathering hub, where one could buy a soft drink, ice cream, a hot dog or another snack and enjoy meeting friends to discuss the news of the day. I spent many Saturday afternoons there as a boy in the 1960s and '70s.

Although the building was torn down, Fishburne Pharmacy still exists today in a different location and is the oldest continually operated business in Waynesboro.

Confederate Veteran magazine published the following obituary after Elliott Fishburne's death in 1906:

Sunday morning, February 25, 1906, after a brief illness, in the sixty-fourth year of his age, Elliott G. Fishburne answered the roll call and his gallant spirit mingled with loved comrades who have crossed over the river and are resting under the shade of the trees.

Headstone of Elliott G. Fishburne, Riverview Cemetery, Waynesboro, Virginia. *Photo by author.*

When Virginia resumed her rightful sovereignty and called her sons to arms, this youth was among the first to respond, and passed from the tender associations and gentle influence of a Christian home into the stern activities of war as a member of Capt. William Patrick's company of cavalry. It was composed for the most part of young men reared in the neighborhood of Waynesboro, Va. This company (afterwards E of the 1st Virginia Cavalry) had no superior in that distinguished regiment, first commanded by Jeb Stuart and afterwards by Fitz Lee. At the reorganization Capt. Patrick was promoted to the rank of major and assigned to the command of the 17th Virginia Battalion. He fell on 29th of August, 1862, but was immortalized by both Jackson and Stuart in their official tribute to his intrepid courage and invaluable services.

For distinguished service Elliott G. Fishburne was promoted to first corporal and then to third sergeant, and twice, at Raccoon Ford and the Wilderness, consecrated with his blood the soil of his loved Virginia. The following is the testimony of M.D. Leonard, a comrade: "We all remember 'Fish' as one who rode at the head of the company. In an engagement his coolness was conspicuous. He knew no fear, as was proven by his conduct on many fields;

Inscription from Elliott G. Fishburne's headstone. *Photo by author.*

but especially on the night after the Second Manassas, when with two comrades, Henry Kennedy and W.S. McCauseland, he captured forty-two well-armed soldiers belonging to a New York cavalry regiment, with the captain at its head, and turned them over as prisoners to the 12th Virginia Cavalry, commanded by Col. A.W. Harrison." Kennedy was killed on this occasion. McCauseland now resides in Texas.

"Ellie" Fishburne's business life after the war was spent in the community where he was born, possessing the love and esteem of those who were his companions in youth. Modesty was his charm, and yet he possessed all the elements of heroic character. His soldier life was a model, and loving memories abide with the comrades who touched elbows with him during those years of trial and sacrifice. His fidelity to all demands of comradeship was abundantly illustrated. He took a lively interest in all Confederate associations. He was ex-President of the Augusta Memorial Association and a member of the Stonewall Jackson Camp, C.V. of Staunton, Va., and his love for cause and comrades seemed to grow stronger with the years. "We shall meet, but we shall miss him." This community *mourns a citizen of character and usefulness. He was laid to rest with military honors. Delegations from the Camp, survivors of Company E, the large attendance of comrades, neighbors, and friends, and the exquisite and lavish floral contribution testified to the affection for his memory. He is survived by a devoted wife, a son, and a daughter.*[230]

Other Fishburnes also made their marks in Waynesboro after the war. Elliott's younger brother, James Abbott Fishburne, was only eleven when the Civil War began.[231] After the war, James attended Washington College while Lee was still president and was heavily influenced by Lee to "devote his life to educating and instilling moral value in future generations."[232]

James would eventually establish Fishburne Military School in Waynesboro in 1879. The school has operated in its current location (just behind where the Confederate army's line was off Pine Avenue, during the Battle of Waynesboro) since 1883. In 1922, the school's yearbook noted, "This school was the apple of Mr. Fishburne's eye, and one of his last conscious utterances was 'a prayer for my boys.'" George Hawke wrote the following about Fishburne:

The school's revered founder, James Abbott Fishburne, died on November 11, 1921—Armistice Day. He had guided the school for forty-two years, maintaining all the while the high moral and ethical standards fostered by Robert E. Lee. His last words were, "God bless my boys." James Fishburne is buried in Riverview Cemetery; a graveside memorial service is held annually by the cadets.[233]

The military boarding school for boys is currently one of only four schools in the United States offering summer Junior ROTC programs that are fully accredited by the United States Army Cadet Command. Both Lee's and Fishburne's positive influence is enduring. They would be pleased.

After the war was over, William Bowen Gallaher returned home to Waynesboro, farmed and managed some the family's business affairs. The 1870 census listed his occupation as farmer. He died on February 19, 1911, and is buried at Riverview Cemetery in Waynesboro. His son, William B. Gallaher Jr., would become a successful surveyor and engineer in Waynesboro, overseeing much of the commercial and residential development of Waynesboro during the 1920s.

Brother DeWitt Clinton Gallaher went back to school after the war, graduating from the University of Virginia in 1868. He married Florence

Walton Miller on July 27, 1876, and practiced law in Roanoke, Virginia, until 1898, later moving to Charleston, West Virginia. He died in Charleston on Christmas Day 1926 and is buried at Spring Hill Cemetery in Charleston.

While the practical aspects of moving on and recovering after the South's defeat occupied most of the energies of southerners in the decades following the war, remembrance was also a very important aspect of that recovery. There was a sense of duty and obligation to remember the sacrifices of the sons, fathers and brothers who had marched so optimistically off to war in the spring of 1861, only to return to, in the words of veteran H.H. Kerr, find "the home he left so beautiful in blackened ruins...his stock killed...his money of no value, and a system of reconstruction which made the horrors of war pale into insignificance."[234]

That sense of duty often manifested itself in the erecting of monuments, statues, highway markers, plaques and other memorials that dot the South's landscape to this day. One such monument was the one erected in honor of Colonel William Harman. It was placed to remind us of his sacrifice

Colonel William H. Harman monument, Constitution Park, Waynesboro, Virginia. *Photo by author.*

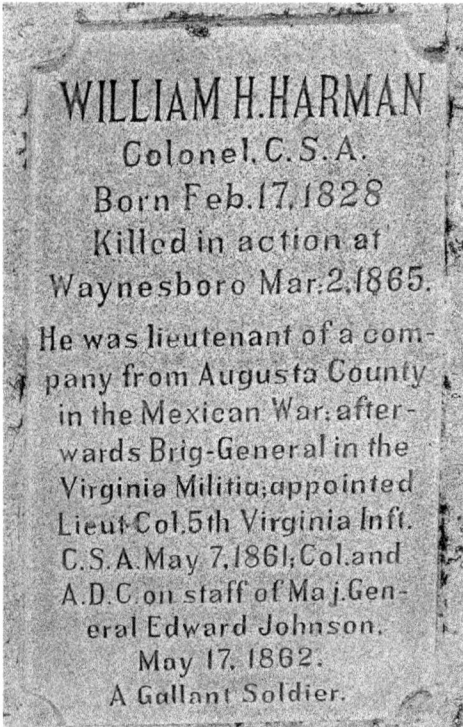

Harman monument text. *Photo by author.*

WILLIAM H.HARMAN
Colonel. C.S.A.
Born Feb.17,1828
Killed in action at
Waynesboro Mar.2,1865.
He was lieutenant of a com-
pany from Augusta County
in the Mexican War; after-
wards Brig-General in the
Virginia Militia;appointed
Lieut-Col.5th Virginia Inft.
C.S.A.May 7,1861,Col.and
A.D.C on staff of Maj.Gen-
eral Edward Johnson.
May 17, 1862.
A Gallant Soldier.

and as a testament to his bravery and commitment in defending his native sod—the very town in which he was born. In 1926, this monument was erected by the Jeb Stuart Chapter (Staunton) of the United Daughters of the Confederacy near the very place of his death. Since that time, this monument has been moved several times and now rests in Waynesboro's Constitution Park, about 550 yards southeast of where he fell. The inscription on the monument reads:

> *William H. Harman*
> *Colonel, C.S.A.*
> *Born Feb. 17, 1828*
> *Killed in action at*
> *Waynesboro Mar 2, 1865.*
> *He was a lieutenant of a com-*
> *pany from Augusta County*
> *in the Mexican War; after-*
> *wards Brig. General in the*
> *Virginia Militia; appointed*
> *Lieut Col. 5th Virginia Inft.*
> *C.S.A. May 7, 1861; Col. and*
> *A.D.C. on staff of Maj. Gen-*
> *eral Edward Johnson.*
> *May 17, 1862.*
> *A Gallant Soldier.*

The fact that Harman's monument has been moved several times and now rests in a rather obscure and hard-to-see location is, in many ways, illustrative of the fading memory and focus regarding the commemoration and memory of the Civil War. I doubt that many local residents even know it exists or are aware of the struggle that took place on the ground that today hosts the stately homes of the now quiet and quaint Tree Streets. In some ways, I believe that those old veterans might be pleased with that. While I do not believe they would want us to forget their sacrifice for duty's sake in the defense of their homes, the fading memory of succeeding generations is a natural outcome of their successful efforts to rebuild the South and unite the country after the war's devastation. I believe many rank and file veterans simply wanted—for themselves and their posterity—a return to some semblance of normalcy. That would not be truly possible without the fading of memory. They wanted the death and destruction to cease. They wanted once again to till their land, sleep under their own roofs, support their families, educate their sons and daughters and worship their God. They wanted to rebuild, reconcile and reunite. And they did. Although that process was halting and imperfect—especially for those new citizens who were no longer slaves—we can remember and honor the men on both sides of that epic conflict for what they did after the war as much as for what they did during the war.

Yet while memories will fade, we should never let them die completely. I believe we should—and will—continue to teach our children and grandchildren what our fathers and mothers and grandparents have taught us and passed down for generations. We will continue to share our family history around the supper table as we eat harvest that was grown and nourished from the very soil that contains the blood of our kin—blood that was shed while defending their homes. We will continue to share our family history on the front porches of our homes in the fading light of summer evenings surrounded by great trees that were present when our ancestors lived. We will continue to share our family history before a crackling fire in our homes on cold winter nights with our children and grandchildren gathered close around us. We will continue to share the stories, the sadness, the injustices, the glory, the bravery, the love, the patriotism, the loyalty and the sacrifices of those who have gone before us. We do this, in part, so that we might "honor our fathers," as the scriptures command us. And we pray that our children and our grandchildren will do the same when their turn comes.

MARIA LEWIS

A Woman of Color in the 8ᵗʰ New York Cavalry?

By Dr. Anita L. Henderson

Note: The following article is included in this book for two reasons. First of all, it is not something with which I (nor any historian I've spoken with) am familiar. Although the information and details are quite limited, it adds a new twist and discovery regarding details about the Battle of Waynesboro that previously have not been published or were even widely known. Secondly, I hope that by exposing the limited information to those interested in the Battle of Waynesboro, some reader may know something or will be able to provide Dr. Henderson with more information or a lead that could fill in additional details about Maria Lewis and possibly confirm her identity.

The early research that I undertook to find a historical basis for my living history portrayal of a woman in uniform who fought in the Civil War led me to a discovery at the Virginia Historical Society. The implications of that discovery are, from a historical and societal perspective, quite amazing.

During my research, I found out about Maria Lewis—a black woman who allegedly rode in disguise with the 8ᵗʰ New York Cavalry during the Civil War. Her existence was initially discovered by Mike Miller at the Alexandria, Virginia library more than ten years ago. The diary (covering a fifty-year period) of a Quaker abolitionist from Rochester, New York, named Julia Wilbur chronicled her own war experiences as she helped with contraband relief efforts in Alexandria. During this time, Wilbur encountered Maria Lewis. Lewis was part of a contingent of soldiers delivering captured

Image of Julia Wilbur's diary entry for April 4, 1865. *Courtesy Dr. Anita Henderson.*

battle flags to the War Department. Who this woman was, why she was fighting and how she enlisted in the Union army are all questions I have been researching over the last several years. Admittedly, the evidence is scant: just four sentences recorded in Wilbur's diary on April 4, 1865, are the only evidence of Lewis's existence. From this limited information, I have attempted to determine this woman's male alias and the circumstances of her enlistment in the Union army.

Julia Wilbur's diary entry of April 4, 1865, reads:

> *Colored woman here who has been 18 months in the 8th NY Cav. _____*
> *Maria Lewis. Wore uniform & carried sword & carbine & rode & scouted*
> *& skirmished & fought like the rest. She comes to W. [Washington,*
> *D.C.] with the men who presented the 17 flags to the War Dept. We shall*
> *see that she has good place.*[235]

At first, the paucity of information seems daunting, but using deductive reasoning and process of elimination, I have been able to narrow down a list of 2,400 troopers who served over four years with the 8th New York to fewer than 5 possible soldiers.

Proceeding with such information requires a framework on which to build. By using the process of asking who, what, when, why and how, one can build a thesis. Facts then begin to emerge that will either support or contradict your working theory. That is the process I've used over the last several years to try to identify Maria Lewis.

Who Was Maria Lewis?

We have only limited information as to this woman's identity. She was most likely a free black woman from the Rochester, New York area. This is the region from which the 8th New York Cavalry was drawn. She had to have been fair-skinned enough to pass for either a white or Native American male. There is a Seneca reservation near Rochester, and a number of them served with the different Rochester regiments. Union regiments were segregated, except in the western theater, so if she were darker-skinned, she would have been prevented from enlisting.

Who Was Julia Wilbur?

Julia Wilbur was a Quaker abolitionist who was sent to Alexandria, Virginia, by the Society of Friends in Rochester to help out with contraband relief efforts there. She kept a fifty-year diary and was witness to important events and people in Washington, D.C., during the Civil War. She rented a room from a free black man in Alexandria and had dealings with Secretary of War Edwin Stanton. She apparently did not hold Stanton in high regard, referring to him as a "pompous ass." Regardless of her relationship with Stanton, Wilbur's mention of Lewis should be considered credible, as she was a well-respected woman in abolitionist circles. As the online introduction to her papers notes:

> *Julia Wilbur (1815–1895) was born near Rochester, NY. The family was of middle-class Quaker background. Mary L. Van Buskirk is probably*

Wilbur's sister. Unmarried, Wilbur taught school in the Rochester public school system. Her diaries indicate an interest in political and social issues, but no one single event brought her to involvement in the abolitionist movement, though she mentions hearing Frederick Douglass speak for the first time in July 1845. She met Harriet Jacobs, a slave who had escaped to the north, in a reading room run by the Rochester Ladies' Anti Slavery Society. Thirteen years later, they would become close friends working together to assist the freed slaves in Alexandria, Virginia.

At the age of 43, Julia Wilbur gave up teaching to care for her niece, Freda, until Freda's father took her to live with him. After a two-year bout with depression, Wilbur relocated to Alexandria, Virginia to assist freed slaves. Here, she distributed food, clothing and supplies to the Contrabands, organized schools, set up orphanages and solicited financial support. After this work was completed, she moved to Washington, D.C. and worked for women's suffrage.

The diaries "have rare and detailed information about Washington's elite black community and about former slaves. They include marvelous detail about life in a city rocked by the political and social upheavals of the war, about nascent racial segregation and about the nature of friendships among black and white women...an extraordinary resource for historians of women, African Americans, Washington and the second half of the 19th century."[236]

Wilbur's diary is the only primary source I've been able to find to date that documents the existence of Maria Lewis. The diary should also be considered a credible source, as it records information and events in real time. Moreover, it is generally true that people are more candid and honest when writing in diaries and journaling—unlike memoirs written thirty years after an event, when memories have faded and other events have shaped those memories. For these reasons, the accuracy and reliability of diaries often lend them more credibility than other types of war recollections and memoirs.

What Was the 8ᵗʰ New York Cavalry?

The 8th New York Cavalry was a three-year volunteer unit from Rochester and the surrounding eight counties. The unit formed in November 1861 and mustered out in June 1865. The soldiers took part in all of the major engagements of the Cavalry Corps of the Army of the Potomac. They escaped the siege of Harper's Ferry under their capable commander, Colonel Benjamin "Grimes" Davis, before the town was captured by Stonewall Jackson during the Antietam Campaign. The 8th was the first regiment to cross the river and strike the Confederate cavalry at Brandy Station, where their beloved commander was killed. They were with Buford holding the Chambersburg Pike on the first day of Gettysburg. They fought in the tough campaigns of 1864, including the Overland, Petersburg and Shenandoah Campaigns. Their divisional commanders included John O. Buford and James Wilson, and they finished their service under General George Armstrong Custer when he took over the division just prior to Cedar Creek. Custer admired the 8th for its hard fighting spirit, and the admiration was mutual, with the regiment quickly becoming "Red Tie Boys."

WHAT?

What is the significance of the seventeen flags? When I first read the mention of the captured flags, it didn't mean anything to me. I found helpful information about the battle in the *Official Records, Custer Victorious: The Civil War Battles of General George Armstrong Custer* and other regimental history books, but once again, there was no mention of Maria Lewis. The *OR* report as recorded by Major Compson of the 8th describes the action at Waynesboro:

> *Moved with the Cavalry Corps from Winchester, Va., February 27, 1865. Were not engaged until March 2, when we met the enemy, under Lieutenant General Early, at Waynesborough. Remained in position about one hour and a half, when we were ordered to charge them. The charge was made, driving the enemy from his position, completely routing and demoralizing them, and capturing as follows, viz: Brigadier General Wharton, C. S. Army, 3 colonels, and upward of 50 other officers of inferior grade, 700–900 noncommissioned officers, and privates, 5 pieces of artillery with caissons, and c., upward of 200 wagons and ambulances, 9 portable forges, 1,200–1,500 stand of small-arms, upward of 900 single sets of harness, upward of 800 team horses and mules, and 10 battle flags; camping that night at Brooksville.*[237]

The answer to the seventeen flags' significance can be found in Greg Urwin's *Custer Victorious:*

The Eight New York and another regiment slashed through the running mob, crossing the South River and then turned around and formed line, cutting off further retreat. The whole action from the time the 3rd Cavalry Division reached Waynesboro to that final charge, lasted only three hours, but when it was over, the last Confederate army in the Shenandoah Valley was utterly destroyed…A few minutes later, Custer led his flushed and smiling Red Ties back to Sheridan. Behind the beaming boy rode seventeen proud troopers, each holding the flags they had captured from the Confederates.[238]

I then wondered if Lewis might have captured one of the flags. If so, did she win the Medal of Honor? There is no evidence that she did. Most of the 8th New York Medal of Honor winners from Waynesboro are line and noncommissioned officers. It would have been highly unlikely for a disguised woman to have been in any command position. This would have made the chance of being discovered more likely.

Where?

There are four main geographic locations that provide clues in helping to determine Lewis's identity:

- Rochester, New York, was the location of an important black community that numbered close to one thousand people out of a total population of forty-nine thousand. It was the home of well-known abolitionist Frederick Douglass, who also published the antislavery *North Star* newspaper. The community was also an important stop on the Underground Railroad. Abolitionist Harriet Tubman also owned a home in the Rochester area. If this black woman joined a Rochester-based cavalry volunteer unit, it would be likely that she would have received encouragement—at least in spirit—from the abolitionist sentiment in the community.

- Julia Wilbur's boardinghouse in Alexandria, Virginia, was the interim destination of the mounted flag bearers before they presented the standards to the War Department. According to Wilbur's diary, she had friends in the 8th New York Cavalry who had visited her there.

- Battle of Waynesboro maps from various sources, including the *OR*, indicate the placement of the 2nd Brigade (which contained the 8th New York) and its progress during the charge in which the flags were captured. One map also places the 8th (or part of it) guarding an escape route on the east side of the South River.

WHEN?

The years 1863–65 are what I have focused on regarding enlistments and the attempt to find out what male alias Lewis might have used when she joined. Wilbur's diary noted that Lewis had been in the 8th New York Cavalry for eighteen months. Based on this information, she would have enlisted sometime in the latter half of 1863. This narrows down possible identities, as the 8th was a three-year regiment, with most of the men enlisting between 1861 and 1862 and reenlisting in 1864 and 1865. Of the 2,882 men who served over four years, only 50 enlisted in 1863. I have gone through the fifty muster records and have narrowed down the list of subjects to several possibilities. Most soldiers were eliminated, as they weren't there at the end of the war—they were dead, wounded, disabled, POWs or deserters. Some enlistment dates were also too early to match Lewis's time frame of enlistment.

WHY?

Why was this black woman in the 8th New York Cavalry, a predominantly white outfit? If we go back to Rochester, we see that there were about 1,000 black people living there. If we eliminate women, that leaves us with about 490 to 500 males, of whom I would estimate that 150 to 200 were of military age (eighteen to forty-five). Most of the black men in Rochester joined the United States Colored Troops units, such as the 54th and 55th Massachusetts Infantry and the 5th Massachusetts Cavalry. Three of Frederick Douglass's sons joined the 54th and 5th. If she had joined a USCT unit, there was the possibility of her being recognized by her black neighbors. Most women disguised as men in uniform joined in locations where people would not recognize them. So, a light-skinned black woman may have been able to pass as a white or Native American male and be relatively secure in the knowledge that most people in the regiment would not know her.

Why did she join? A lot of women who fought were from the lower and lower-middle classes. Some were escaping bad personal relationships or working conditions. Others joined out of patriotism or adventure. These reasons are explored and chronicled in De Anne Blanton and Lauren Cook's book *They Fought Like Demons: Women Soldiers in the American Civil War.*[239]

There is also the question of how she eluded detection. My working theory, as mentioned, is that she probably passed for a white or Native American male. The Iroquois Confederacy had reservations nearby, and American Indians served in the New York regiments. The concept of race is a social rather than biological one. Many "black" Americans have up to three different gene pools in their ancestry—African, European and/or Indian. Therefore, we run the gamut in terms of physical appearance.

Most physical exams were cursory at best—the recruiting officer/orderly being primarily concerned with checking the mouth for sufficient teeth to tear paper cartridges and making sure that the recruit had a trigger finger.

Maria Lewis's service and identity, assuming that her story is real, are elusive. Her efforts in concealing her identity were evidently well thought out—that identity has been kept secret for 150 years. Years of research has yielded very little. I am nonetheless convinced that there is a letter, a photograph, another diary entry or some other piece of credible evidence that will someday confirm Lewis's identity and her role in the Battle of Waynesboro.

Anita L. Henderson, MD, was born in Chicago, Illinois. She obtained her BA degree from Wellesley College and her MD degree from Howard University College of Medicine. She has been in private practice in dermatology in Columbia, Maryland, for thirty years. She has had a lifelong love of horses and history and learned how to ride at age seven. Besides participating in cavalry reenactments, she has played polo, driven on carriage drives, conducted trail rides, participated in fox hunts and also does cowboy mounted shooting. Her love of riding was a contributing factor in her wanting to do a cavalry impression in Civil War reenacting when she started in 1998. Discovering Maria Lewis gave her the historical basis to do this more accurately.

She is a functional mounted cavalry bugler with the 13th Virginia Cavalry, Company H, Light Sussex Dragoons, which had two documented black Confederates who were duly mustered in. She recently was chief confederate bugler of the 150th Blue-Gray Alliance Gettysburg Reenactment in June 2013. She also has a civilian impression and is a longtime member of the Atlantic Guard Soldiers' Aid Society, one of the most authentic civilian living history groups in the United States. She does an impression of a house slave or free black woman who is a cook and demonstrates open fire and hearth cooking using nineteenth-century recipes and implements.

Dr. Henderson has participated in living history interpretations and reenactments all over the East Coast and southern United States. She has participated in a variety of historical documentary and Hollywood films. She was a background artist in the Civil War films Wicked Spring, No Retreat from Destiny and Gods and Generals. In addition to interpreting the Civil War, she is an avid genealogist and is descended from the Egglestons of Virginia and Mississippi. She is currently working on the family history with distant white cousins who are also avid Civil War scholars and genealogists. Dr. Henderson lives in rural western Howard County, Maryland, where she enjoys riding her pony, Fuzzy; gardening; writing; and milking her goat, Butter.

Any reader having clues to the mystery of Maria Lewis is encouraged to contact Dr. Henderson at agintomboy@aol.com.

NOTES

INTRODUCTION

1. Johnson, *Douglas Southall Freeman*, 55–56.
2. Gallagher, *Confederate War*, 13.
3. Freeman, *South to Posterity*, xix.
4. Wert, *Brotherhood of Valor*, 15.

CHAPTER 1

5. Hawke, *History of Waynesboro*, 40.
6. A 112,000-acre tract granted to William Beverly by the colonial government.
7. De Beauvoir, *Travels in North America*, 242.
8. The other unit was an infantry company formed by Captain William Long. This unit later became Company B, 2nd of the 52nd Virginia, and was known as the "Waynesboro Guards."
9. *Augusta County Historical Bulletin* 10, no. 1, "Early Civil War Days in Waynesboro."
10. Ibid., 13–15.
11. Driver, *1st Virginia Cavalry*, 214.
12. Augusta County, Virginia soldiers' records, Valley of the Shadow, http://valley.lib.virginia.edu/govdoc/soldiers_dossier.html.

13. Wert, *Brotherhood of Valor*, 13–14.
14. *Augusta County Historical Bulletin* 10, no. 1, "Early Civil War Days in Waynesboro," 15.
15. Ibid., 16.
16. The Crozet Tunnel, an engineering marvel in its day, lay just to the east of Waynesboro. It was built by Claudius Crozet and ran under Afton Mountain of the Blue Ridge. Although Hugh Gallaher did not work on the tunnel, his eldest son, William, was the first man to crawl through the opening upon its completion on Christmas Day 1856. Going through solid granite using only hand drills and black powder, the tunnel was less than six inches off center when completed. Stonewall Jackson used the tunnel to march his "foot cavalry" through and avoid detection by the Union army. I went through the abandoned tunnel (twice) as a boy in the 1970s. There is a current effort underway to reopen the tunnel as a bike and hiking path.
17. The material on the Gallaher family—letters, diaries and articles—takes up most of a complete file cabinet drawer at the Waynesboro Public Library.
18. For many years, Pastor Richardson conducted a classical school in Waynesboro. Many of the young men who marched off to war from Waynesboro had been his students.
19. Gallaher, *Diary*, 12. DeWitt C. Gallaher Jr. notes in the foreword to this work that his father compiled the "booklet" in 1919 from "memo books and scraps of paper he had managed to conserve; all depicting his wartime experiences."
20. The Southern Claims Commission was created by the U.S. government in 1871 so southerners could file claims for property confiscated by the Union army during the Civil War. In order to qualify for reimbursement, claimants had to prove that they held Unites States citizenship, had resided in the seceded state, had their property taken in an "official" capacity and not by looters and had remained loyal to the Union during the war and were not Confederate sympathizers. Roughly two-thirds of all claims filed were denied. From 1871 to 1879, there were 137 claims submitted from Augusta County, Virginia (including Waynesboro). Of those, 36 were approved.
21. Hawke, "Hugh Gallaher," 1.
22. Ibid., Appendix A.
23. Ibid., 21.
24. Hawke, *History of Waynesboro*, 155.

25. "The Academy," as it was known by locals, was constructed in 1832 and served as Waynesboro's first town hall, as well as a school. It was also utilized as a hospital during the Civil War.

26. Gallaher, *Diary*, 5.

27. William B. Gallaher to his father, April 20, 1861, letter, Valley of the Shadow, "Letters of William B. Gallaher, 1861," http://vshadow.vcdh.virginia.edu/cwgallaherlist.html.

28. William B. Gallaher to his mother, May 23, 1861, letter, Valley of the Shadow, "Letters of William B. Gallaher, 1861," http://vshadow.vcdh.virginia.edu/cwgallaherlist.html.

29. William B. Gallaher to his mother, undated, letter, Valley of the Shadow, "Letters of William B. Gallaher, 1861," http://vshadow.vcdh.virginia.edu/cwgallaherlist.html.

30. Ibid.

31. William B. Gallaher to his father, July 22, 1861, letter, Valley of the Shadow, "Letters of William B. Gallaher, 1861," http://vshadow.vcdh.virginia.edu/cwgallaherlist.html.

32. William B. Gallaher to his mother, August 8, 1861, letter, Valley of the Shadow, "Letters of William B. Gallaher, 1861," http://vshadow.vcdh.virginia.edu/cwgallaherlist.html.

33. Hawke, "Hugh Gallaher," 9–10.

34. Ibid., 4.

35. Ibid., 5.

36. Ibid., 10–11.

37. Ibid., 70–71.

38. Robinson, *Confederate Privateers*, 255–56.

39. Hawke, "Hugh Gallaher," 79.

40. Ibid., 79–80.

41. Ibid., 80.

42. Robinson, *Confederate Privateers*, 310.

43. Hawke, "Hugh Gallaher," 80.

44. Ibid., 83.

45. Ibid.

CHAPTER 2

46. Early, *Lieutenant General Jubal Anderson Early*, xvii–xviii.

47. Ibid., xix.

48. Ibid.
49. Ibid., xxii.
50. Wise, *End of an Era*, 228.
51. Ibid.
52. Early, *Lieutenant General Jubal Anderson Early*, xxiv.
53. Tagg, *Generals of Gettysburg*, 256.
54. Early, *Lieutenant General Jubal Anderson Early*, vii.
55. Ibid., vii–viii.
56. Early, *Memoir of the Last Year*, 123.
57. *The War of the Rebellion: A Compilation of the Official Records of the Union and Confederate Armies*, series 1, vol. 43, part 2, 202 (hereafter *OR*).
58. *OR*, series 1, vol. 46, 386.
59. Baker, *Civil War Memoirs*, 17.
60. Curtis Bowman, "Days of Yore: Grant Had Eye on Valley during Civil War," *Waynesboro News-Virginian*, March 8, 1997, A-5.
61. *OR*, series 1, vol. 46, 413.
62. Heatwole, *The Burning*.
63. Early, *Lieutenant General Jubal Anderson Early*, 459.

CHAPTER 3

64. Although Sheridan was in command of the Union forces engaged at Waynesboro, he would remain in Staunton, about fifteen miles west, and would trust the overall prosecution of the battle to his capable lieutenant, George A. Custer.
65. Sheridan claimed different dates and places of birth during his lifetime. The date cited is the most commonly accepted one.
66. Larke, *Life of Gen. P.H. Sheridan*, 18–19.
67. Burr and Hinton, *"Little Phil" and His Troopers*, 27.
68. Ibid.
69. William R. Terrill had three brothers who fought for the Confederacy, two of whom were killed during the war. William was disowned by his family, and according to legend, William's father placed a monument to his slain sons that read, "This monument erected by their father. God alone knows which was right."
70. Hutton, *Phil Sheridan and His Army*, 5.
71. Sheridan, *Personal Memoirs*, vol. 1, 11–12.
72. Hutton, *Phil Sheridan and His Army*, 4.

73. Greiner, *General Phil Sheridan as I Knew Him*, 353.

74. Sheridan, *Personal Memoirs*, vol. 1, 11–12.

75. Faulkner, *Life of Philip Henry Sheridan*, 137.

76. Kenneth E. Koons, "Our Once Beautiful but Now Desolated Valley: Farming in the Breadbasket of the Confederacy," Shenandoah Valley Civil War History and Battlefields Foundation, www.shenandoahatwar.org/the-History/the-Stories/our-once-beautiful-but-now-desolated-valley.

77. *OR*, series 1, vol. 43, part 1, 916.

78. Ibid., 1, vol. 37, part 2, 366.

79. Sheridan, *Personal Memoirs*, vol. 1, 11–12.3.

80. John Heatwole, "The Burning: 'The Fire and Sword of War,'" Shenandoah Valley Civil War History and Battlefields Foundation, www.shenandoahatwar.org/the-history/the-stories/the-burning-the-fire-and-sword-of-war.

81. In the author's experience, even in recent years, one will still occasionally come across lingering resentment in Shenandoah Valley families whose ancestors suffered at the hands of Sheridan's army during the fall of 1864.

82. Heatwole, *The Burning*, 96.

83. Ibid., 97.

84. Ibid., 150–51.

85. Greiner, *General Phil Sheridan as I Knew Him*, 7.

86. Ibid., 314.

87. Heatwole, *The Burning*, xi.

88. Kidd, *Personal Recollections*, 399.

89. Heatwole, *The Burning*, 45–46.

90. Douglas, *I Rode with Stonewall*, 315–16

91. *OR*, series 1, vol. 43, part 1, 30–31.

92. PBS, New Perspectives on the West, "Philip Henry Sheridan," http://www.pbs.org/weta/thewest/people/s_z/sheridan.htm.

CHAPTER 4

93. *OR*, series 1, vol. 37, part 1, 96.

94. Waddell, *Waddell's Annals of Augusta County*, 498.

95. Hawke, *History of Waynesboro*, 114.

96. Lloyd, "Battle of Waynesboro," 194.

97. Waddell, *Waddell's Annals of Augusta County*, 498.

98. Ibid., 500.

99. Berkeley, *Four Years in the Confederate Artillery*, 117.

100. Ibid., 121.

101. Macon, Macon and Macon, *Reminiscences of the Civil War*, 122.

102. Davis, *51ˢᵗ Virginia Infantry*, 40.

103. Lloyd, "Battle of Waynesboro," 195, 197.

104. The Shenandoah River, which divides much of the lower Valley, flows south–north before meeting the Potomac at Harper's Ferry—hence the "lower" and "upper" references, with "lower" designating the northern end of the Valley and "upper" designating the southern end.

105. *OR*, series 1, vol. 46, part 1, 475.

106. Early, *Memoir of the Last Year*, 124.

107. Unsourced article, "Mrs. Whitlock Tells Story of Local Unknown Soldier," Waynesboro Heritage Foundation Museum Battle of Waynesboro file.

108. Sheridan, *Personal Memoirs*, vol. 2, 114.

109. Ibid., 114–15.

110. Wise, *Long Arm of Lee*, 920.

111. Early, *Memoir of the Last Year*, 124.

112. Ibid., note on page 104.

113. West, *30ᵗʰ Battalion Virginia Sharpshooters*, 202.

114. Lloyd, "Battle of Waynesboro," 199.

115. Nicholas, *Sheridan's James River Campaign*, 87–88.

116. Wise, *Long Arm of Lee*, 878.

117. Berkeley, *Four Years in the Confederate Artillery*, xvi–xvii.

118. Wise, *Long Arm of Lee*, 912.

119. Lloyd, "Battle of Waynesboro," 199.

120. *Daily Charlotte Observer*, July 13, 1877, 1.

121. Longacre, *Cavalry at Gettysburg*, 51.

122. Lloyd, "Battle of Waynesboro," 195–96.

123. Ibid., 196.

124. Ibid., 196–97.

125. Gallaher, *Diary*, 22.

126. Lloyd, "Battle of Waynesboro," 200.

127. Ibid.

128. From a letter reproduced from *OR*, series 1, vol. 46, 502.

129. *OR*, series 1, vol. 46, part 1, 516.

130. Ibid.

131. Forsberg, *Memoir*.

132. Early, *Memoir of the Last Year*, 102.

133. Lloyd, "Battle of Waynesboro," 200–201, 207–8.

134. Ibid., 201.

135. Although Sheridan's available force numbered almost 10,000 soldiers, there were only about 2,500 who actually participated in the battle.

136. Withrow, "Pages of Memory."

137. Berkeley, *Four Years in the Confederate Artillery*, 121.

138. There are conflicting accounts on both the number of Confederate artillery pieces involved in the battle and their positions—both in written accounts as well as in maps showing artillery positions. It is the author's opinion that Hotchkiss's reputation for detail should be given special weight when considering the conflicting accounts.

139. *OR*, series 1, vol. 46, part 1, 516.

140. Lloyd, "Battle of Waynesboro," 201.

141. Ibid.

142. From a letter reproduced from *OR*, series 1, vol. 46, 501–4.

143. Lloyd, "Battle of Waynesboro," 202.

144. *Confederate Veteran* 31, no. 13 (1923).

145. *OR*, series 1, vol. 46, 501–4.

146. Ibid.

147. Major General (USA) James H. Wilson to Brigadier General Alexander B. Dyer, January 2, 1865, *OR*, series 1, vol. 45, part 2, 488.

148. Starr, *Union Cavalry in the Civil War*, 373.

149. *OR*, series 1, vol. 46, part 1, 516.

150. Moore, *Gibraltar of the Shenandoah*, 135.

151. Lloyd, "Battle of Waynesboro," 202–3.

152. Early, *Memoir of the Last Year*, 463.

153. Ibid.

154. Ibid.

155. Ibid.

156. From a letter reproduced from *OR*, series 1, vol. 46, 501–4.

157. Berkeley, *Four Years in the Confederate Artillery*, 122.

158. Ibid.

159. Ibid.

160. Gallaher, *Diary*, 24–25.

161. Ibid., 24.

162. Ibid., 25.

163. *Waynesboro News-Virginian*, "Monument on Main Street Pays Tribute to Gen. Harman and City's Part in History," October 31, 1949.

164. Dewitt Clinton Gallaher, "The Death of Col. Wm. H. Harman," *Valley Virginian*, October 15, 1926. *Virginian* articles available at the Valley of the Shadow Project, http://valley.lib.virginia.edu.

165. The text of this letter is included in a hardbound collection of copies of magazine and newspaper articles about the Battle of Waynesboro. The collection is titled *Battle of Waynesboro*, with no publisher or editor noted. It was bound in 1997. Two copies are on hand at the Waynesboro Public Library.

166. The account referred to by Woods, and written by DeWitt Clinton Gallaher, differs slightly from Woods's recounting of Harman's death. Gallaher had written in an earlier newspaper article (date unavailable but prior to 1885) that Harman's body had been "removed to a storeroom in the Withrow property." Both the Woods and Withrow properties were on the south side of Main Street, so confusing the two "storerooms" is understandable. But since Gallaher did not actually witness Harman's death (his diary notes that he was not directly involved in the battle but rather "entered the town [as] the last of the Yankees were leaving en-route to Charlottesville"), Woods's accounting as an eyewitness should be taken as the more reliable of the two. Moreover, Gallaher's recounting states that he viewed Harman's body "the day after he was killed." So it's possible that Harman's body was moved from the Woods storeroom to a storeroom on the Withrow property. Gallaher also wrote in this account that "[m]y recollection is…," giving the reader the impression that Gallaher was not recalling the details with absolute certainty.

167. Early, *Lieutenant General Jubal Anderson Early*, 464.

168. *Republican Vindicator*, March 24, 1865, 2. *Vindicator* articles available at the Valley of the Shadow Project, http://valley.lib.virginia.edu.

169. Ibid.

170. Garber, *Harman-Garber Record*, 100–102.

171. There is one other unconfirmed Confederate casualty that is sometimes confused with Harman's death. In an article in the files at the Waynesboro Heritage Foundation Museum, there is an unsourced and undated account by a "Mrs. Whitlock," who was the "granddaughter of William Alexander, founder of the funeral parlor and furniture shop." The article notes, "It was she who found the body [unknown Confederate soldier] which still lies buried in the Community Cemetery (Presbyterian Cemetery). The wooden cross which once marked the sites of this burial has been gone for a good many years and the exact site of the body is no longer known." The account further states, "It was then, in the front yard of her home, Emma Alexander [Mrs. Whitlock] found a dead horse

and several hundred yards from it, the body of a Confederate soldier. Wounded, he had evidently tried to get into her father's shop before he died, Mrs. Whitlock said." This soldier could be confused with Colonel Harman, except for the conflict of the claim that this "unknown soldier" was buried at the Presbyterian Cemetery—Colonel Harman is buried at Thornrose Cemetery in Staunton, Virginia. See article in Waynesboro Heritage Foundation Museum Battle of Waynesboro file titled "Mrs. Whitlock Tells Story of Local Unknown Soldier."

172. Early, *Memoir of the Last Year*, 103.
173. Gallaher, "Death of Col. Wm. H. Harman."
174. Lloyd, "Battle of Waynesboro," 204.
175. Cause, *Four Years with Five Armies*, 359.
176. Ibid., 361.
177. *OR*, series 1, vol. 46, 503.
178. Early, *Memoir of the Last Year*, note on page 104.
179. Wert, *Custer*, 208.
180. Early, *Memoir of the Last Year*, note on page 104.
181. Ibid., 100.
182. *OR*, vol. 46, 517.
183. Pond, *Army in the Civil War*, 253.
184. Early, *Memoir of the Last Year*, 103.
185. Nicholas, *Sheridan's James River Campaign*, 84.
186. The Medal of Honor citations themselves indicate that fifteen flags were involved, although there is a possible duplication for Early's headquarters flag. I offer my thanks to fellow Virginian and historian Robert Moore for assembling the following list of Medal of Honor recipients for actions at the Battle of Waynesboro: Charles W. Anderson (George Pforr), Private, 1st New York (Lincoln) Cavalry—citation: capture of unknown Confederate flag; Henry H. Bickford, Corporal, Co. E, 8th New York Cavalry—citation: recapture of flag; Christopher C. Bruton/Braton, Captain, Co. C, 22nd New York Cavalry—citation: capture of General Early's headquarters flag, Confederate national standard; Warren Carman, Private, Co. A (or H?), 1st New York (Lincoln) Cavalry—citation: capture of flag and several prisoners; Hartwell B. Compson, Major, 8th New York Cavalry—citation: capture of flag belonging to General Early's headquarters; Michael Crowley, Private, Co. A, 22nd New York Cavalry—citation: capture of flag; Charles Arthur Goheen, First Sergeant, Co. G, 8th New York Cavalry—citation: capture of flag; Harry Harvey, Corporal, Co. A, 22nd New York Cavalry—citation: capture of flag and bearer, with two other prisoners;

Daniel Armer Kelly, Sergeant, Co. G, 8th New York Cavalry—citation: capture of flag; Andrew Kuder, Second Lieutenant, Co. G, 8th New York Cavalry—citation: capture of flag; George Ladd, Private, Co. H, 22nd New York Cavalry—citation: captured a standard bearer, his flag, horse and equipment; James Madison, Sergeant, Co. E, 8th New York Cavalry—citation: recapture of General Crook's headquarters flag; John Miller, Private, Co. H, 8th New York Cavalry—citation: capture of flag; Robert Niven, Second Lieutenant, Co. H, 8th New York Cavalry— citation: capture of two flags; Peter O'Brien, Corporal, Co. A, 1st New York (Lincoln) Cavalry—citation: capture of flag and of a Confederate officer with his horse and equipment.

187. Early, *Memoir of the Last Year*, 103.
188. *Republican Vindicator*, "To the People of Augusta," March 31, 1865.
189. *OR*, series 1, vol. 46, 503.
190. E.W. Whitaker to Charles Green, February 4, 1907, letter printed as a pamphlet by the Michigan Custer Memorial Association, 1907, Custer Collection, Monroe County Historical Society, Monroe, Michigan.
191. Early, *Memoir of the Last Year*, 129.
192. Ibid., 108.
193. Although the phrase first appeared in Edward A. Pollard's 1866 book *The Lost Cause: A New Southern History of the War of the Confederates*, it is Early whom most historians credit with establishing the Lost Cause perspective as an intellectual and literary movement and school of thought that dominated the South (and influenced the North) for more than one hundred years. Although considered discredited by some modern historians, aspects of the perspective still retain much of their influence today—both in popular history and among some academics and Civil War historians.
194. Gallagher and Nolan, *Myth of the Lost Cause*, 36.
195. Early, *Memoir of the Last Year*, 130.
196. Civil War Trust, "Philip Sheridan," http://www.civilwar.org/education/history/biographies/phillip-sheridan.html.

Chapter 5

197. United States Department of the Interior, National Park Service, *National Register of Historic Places Registration Form—Plumb House*, December 17, 1990.

198. John Alfred Plumb, Sarah Ann Doggett (Plumb) and Margaret Aliese Leslie (Plumb), "The Plumb House: History and Its People," John Plumb's personal papers, 5.

199. Ibid.

200. Personal correspondence from John Plumb.

Chapter 6

201. Pollard, *Southern History of the War*, 109.

202. Freeman, *R.E. Lee*, 490.

203. Ibid., 526.

204. *Valley Virginian*, "The Freshet at Home," October 6, 1870, 3.

205. *Staunton Vindicator*, "Details of the Freshet. Immense Destruction of Property," October 7, 1870, 2.

206. Hawke, *History of Waynesboro*, 129.

207. *Staunton Spectator*, "All Should Labor," December 26, 1865. *Spectator* articles available at the Valley of the Shadow Project, http://valley.lib.virginia.edu.

208. Port Republic Road Historic District Registration Form, Virginia Department of Historic Resources, DHR file no. 136-5054, United States Department of the Interior, National Park Service, February 4, 2002, 35.

209. Ibid., 38.

210. Ibid., 38–39.

211. Ibid., 40.

212. Clark, *Waynesboro's Black Community*, 4–5.

213. Phipps, *William Sheppard*, 2.

214. Ibid., 3.

215. Sheppard, *Presbyterian Pioneers in Congo*, 15.

216. Ibid., 16.

217. Phipps, *William Sheppard*, xii.

218. Clark, *Waynesboro's Black Community*, 14–15.

219. Virginia Metalcrafters, "Virginia Metalcrafters History," http://www.virginiametalcrafters.com/2010/07/14/virginia-metalcrafters-history.

220. The "rank" of colonel might have been an honorary one. It was rather common in the postwar South to refer to older Confederate veterans—particularly those as distinguished as Withrow—as "Colonel." However, Curtis Bowman noted in a November 14, 1992 *News-Virginian* article that a "source stated that he also has served on the staff of General Dearing,

with the rank of lieutenant colonel; however no further details were given about this phase of his wartime experiences. Suffice it to say, his use of the title 'colonel' in later years appears to have been legitimate." Bowman does not disclose this other source.

221. Cashin, *History of Augusta College*, 13.

222. *Confederate Veteran* 29 (January 1921): 347.

223. C.H. Withrow obituary, *Augusta* [GA] *Chronicle*, n.d., author's collection.

224. Curtis Bowman, "Days of Yore, Charles Withrow's Career Was a 'Class Act,'" *Waynesboro News-Virginian*, November 14, 1992.

225. *United States Department of the Interior, National Park Service, National Register of Historic Places Registration Form—Tree Streets Historic District*, April 12, 2002, 80.

226. Bowman, *Waynesboro Days of Yore*, vol. 1, 132.

227. Ibid.

228. R.G. Williams to Mr. Curtis L. Bowman, August 25, 1986, letter, author's personal collection. My father recounted this same story to me on numerous occasions as well. I've had some individuals express doubt to me that the horse my father recalls feeding with his grandfather could be the same horse, Bird—this due to the fact that my father wasn't born until 1935, and Withrow died in 1921. That doubt is understandable. However, since a horse's average life span is twenty to twenty-five years (and even thirty is not that uncommon), there really isn't any reason to doubt the account. Even if the horse was ten when Withrow passed, adding twenty more years to that date would make my father about six years of age and Bird thirty—certainly within the realm of possibility.

229. Department of Confederate Military Affairs, "Re-Union, Co. E, 1ˢᵗ Va. Cavalry," 8.

230. *Confederate Veteran* 14, no. 5 (May 1906): 221–22.

231. Fishburne Military Academy's website makes the following claim about its founder: "During the Civil War, Professor Fishburne served as a drummer under General Robert E. Lee" (http://www.fishburne.org/page.cfm?p=445). While that is possible, his age casts some doubt, as does an article in an *Augusta Historical Bulletin* published in the fall of 1988 that mentions "the vivid impression the battle made on 14-year-old James Abbott Fishburne, as he watched from his Main Street home." *Augusta Historical Bulletin* 24, no. 2, 15.

232. Hawke, *History of Waynesboro*, 85.

233. Ibid., 87.

234. Department of Confederate Military Affairs, "Re-Union, Co. E, 1ˢᵗ Va. Cavalry," 8.

APPENDIX

235. Wilbur, *Diary*.

236. Haverford College Library, Julia Wilbur Papers, "Biographical Note," http://www.haverford.edu/library/special/aids/wilbur_julia/wilbur1158.pdf.

237. *OR*, series 1, vol. 46, part 1, "Appomattox Campaign," number 10, *Report of Major Hartwell B. Compson, 8th New York Cavalry, 2nd Brigade*, report of operations of the 8th New York Cavalry during the late expedition.

238. Urwin, *Custer Victorious*, 229–30.

239. See Blanton and Cook, *They Fought Like Demons*.

BIBLIOGRAPHY

PRIMARY SOURCES

Augusta County Historical Society Archives, Staunton, Virginia.

Baker, Isaac Norval. *Civil War Memoirs, 18ᵗʰ Virginia Cavalry, Company F. (Imboden's Brigade)*. Lexington: Virginia Military Institute Archives, n.d.

Berkeley, Henry Robinson. *Four Years in the Confederate Artillery.* Edited by William H. Runge. Richmond: Virginia Historical Society, 1991.

Burr, Frank A., and Richard J. Hinton. *"Little Phil" and His Troopers: The Life of Gen. Philip H. Sheridan.* New York: Hurst & Company, 1890.

Cause, Isaac. *Four Years with Five Armies.* New York: Neale Publishing Company, 1908.

De Beauvoir, François Jean, Marquis de Chastellux. *Travels in North America in the Years 1780-81-82*. New York: White, Gallaher & White, 1827.

Department of Confederate Military Affairs. "Re-Union, Co. E, 1ˢᵗ Va. Cavalry, Waynesboro, Virginia, April 19, 2011." Cavalry Unit Records, Accession 27684, Box 14, Folder 5.

Douglas, Henry Kyd. *I Rode with Stonewall.* Chapel Hill: University of North Carolina Press, 1940.

Early, Jubal. *Lieutenant General Jubal Anderson Early C.S.A. AUTOBIOGRAPHICAL SKETCH AND NARRATIVE OF THE WAR BETWEEN THE STATES.* Philadelphia: J.B. Lippincott Company, 1912.

———. *A Memoir of the Last Year of the War for Independence in the Confederate States of America, Containing an Account of the Operations of His Commands in the Years 1864 and 1865.* Lynchburg, VA: Charles W. Button, 1867.

Faulkner, Joseph. *The Life of Philip Henry Sheridan: The Dashing, Brave and Successful Soldier.* New York: Hurst & Company Publishers, 1888.

Forsberg, Augustus. *Memoir.* N.p., circa 1870. Available at Leyburn Library, Special Collections, Washington and Lee University, Lexington, Virginia.

Gallaher, DeWitt Clinton. *A Diary—Depicting the Experiences of DeWitt Clinton Gallaher in the War Between the States While Serving in the Confederate Army.* Charleston, WV: DeWitt C. Gallaher Jr., 1945.

Garber, Virginia Armistead. *Harman-Garber Record.* Charlottesville, VA: William Harman Surber, 1926.

Greiner, H.C. *General Phil Sheridan as I Knew Him, Playmate—Comrade—Friend.* Chicago: J.S. Hyland and Company, 1908.

Haverford College Library, Special Collections. Julia Wilbur Papers. Haverford College, Haverford, Pennsylvania.

Kidd, James Harvey. *Personal Recollections of a Cavalryman with Custer's Michigan Cavalry Brigade in the Civil War.* Ionia, MI: Sentinel Printing Company, 1908.

Larke, Julian K. *The Life of Gen. P.H. Sheridan, the Hero of the Shenandoah.* New York: T.R. Dawley, 1864.

Lloyd, Harlan Page. "The Battle of Waynesboro." In *Sketches of War History, 1861–1865: Papers Prepared for the Ohio Commandery of the Military Order of the*

BIBLIOGRAPHY

Loyal Legion of the United States 1890–96. Vol. 4. Edited by W.H. Chamberlin. Cincinnati, OH: Robert Clarke Company, 1896.

Macon, Emma, Cassandra Riely Macon and Reuben Conway Macon. *Reminiscences of the Civil War.* Cedar Rapids, IA: K.C.M. Paulson, 1911.

Official Records of the Union and Confederate Navies in the War of the Rebellion. Washington, D.C.: Government Printing Office, 1894–1917.

Pollard, E.A. *Southern History of the War: The Last Year of the War.* New York: Charles B. Richardson, 1866.

Pond, George E. *The Army in the Civil War.* Vol. 11 of 16, *The Shenandoah Valley in 1864.* New York: Charles Scribner's Sons, 1885.

Sheppard, William H. *Presbyterian Pioneers in Congo.* Richmond, VA: Presbyterian Committee of Publication, 1927.

Sheridan, Michael V., Brigadier General. *Personal Memoirs of Philip Henry Sheridan, General, United States Army.* Vol. 1. New York: D. Appleton and Company, 1902.

Valley of the Shadow: Two Communities in the American Civil War. University of Virginia Library. http://valley.lib.virginia.edu.

Waddell, Joseph A. *Waddell's Annals of Augusta County, Virginia, from 1726 to 1871.* Staunton, VA: Russell Caldwell, Publisher, 1902.

The War of the Rebellion: A Compilation of the Official Records of the Union and Confederate Armies. 128 vols. Washington, D.C.: Government Printing Office, 1880–1901.

Waynesboro Heritage Foundation and Museum Archives, Waynesboro, Virginia.

Waynesboro Public Library Archives, Waynesboro, Virginia.

Wilbur, Julia. *Julia Wilbur Diary.* Available at the Lloyd House, Alexandria Public Library, Alexandria, Virginia. Original at Haverford College

Library, Special Collections, Julia Wilbur Papers, Haverford College, Haverford, Pennsylvania.

Wise, Jennings Cropper. *The Long Arm of Lee, or The History of the Artillery of the Army of Northern Virginia with a Brief Account of the Confederate Bureau of Ordnance.* Vol. 2. Lynchburg, VA: J.P. Bell Company, 1915.

Wise, John S. *The End of an Era.* Boston: Houghton, Mifflin and Company, 1901.

Withrow, Louisa. "The Pages of Memory." N.d. Available via Waynesboro Heritage Foundation collections.

SECONDARY SOURCES

Augusta County Historical Bulletin 10, no. 2 (Spring 1974); 25, no. 2 (Spring 1989); 24, no. 1 (Fall 1988).

Battle of Waynesboro. Waynesboro, VA: Waynesboro Public Library, 1997.

Blanton, Deanne, and Lauren Cook. *They Fought Like Demons: Women Soldiers in the American Civil War.* Baton Rouge: Louisiana State University Press, 2002.

Bowman, Curtis L., Sr. *Waynesboro Days of Yore.* Vol. 1. Waynesboro, VA: self-published, 1991.

———. *Waynesboro Days of Yore.* Vol. 2. Waynesboro, VA: self-published, 1991.

Cashin, Edward J. *A History of Augusta College.* Augusta, GA: Augusta College Press, 1976.

Clark, Lillian. *Waynesboro's Black Community: Historical Reflections.* Waynesboro, VA: self-published, 1992.

Davis, James A. *51st Virginia Infantry—The Virginia Regimental Histories Series.* Lynchburg, VA: H.E. Howard Inc., 1984.

Driver, Robert J. *1st Virginia Cavalry—The Virginia Regimental Histories Series.* Lynchburg, VA: H.E. Howard Inc., 1991.

Freeman, Douglas Southall. *R.E. Lee: A Biography.* Vol. 4. New York: Charles Scribner's Sons, 1934.

———. *The South to Posterity.* Baton Rouge: Louisiana University Press, 1998.

Gallagher, Gary W. *The Confederate War.* Cambridge, MA: Harvard University Press, 1999.

Gallagher, Gary W., and Alan T. Nolan. *The Myth of the Lost Cause and Civil War History.* Bloomington: Indiana University Press, 2000.

Hawke, George R. *A History of Waynesboro, Virginia to 1900.* Waynesboro, VA: Waynesboro Historical Commission, 1997.

———. "Hugh Gallaher: Yankee or Rebel?" Printed in 1988. Available via Waynesboro Public Library Archives, Waynesboro, Virginia.

Heatwole, John L. *The Burning: Sheridan's Devastation of the Shenandoah Valley.* Charlottesville, VA: Rockbridge Publishing, 1998.

Hutton, Paul Andrew. *Phil Sheridan and His Army.* Norman: University of Oklahoma Press, 1999.

Johnson, David E. *Douglas Southall Freeman.* Gretna, LA: Pelican Publishing Company, 2002.

Longacre, Edward G. *The Cavalry at Gettysburg: A Tactical Study of Mounted Operations during the Civil War's Pivotal Campaign, 9 June–14 July 1863.* Lincoln, NE: Bison Books, 1993.

Massie, Elizabeth Spilman, and Courtney Skinner. *Images of Waynesboro, Virginia.* Charleston, SC: Arcadia Publishing, 2009.

Moore, Robert H. *Gibraltar of the Shenandoah.* Virginia Beach, VA: Donning Company Publishers, 2004.

Nicholas, Richard L. *Sheridan's James River Campaign of 1865.* Scottsville, VA: Historic Albemarle, 2011.

Phipps, William E. *William Sheppard: Congo's African American Livingstone.* Louisville, KY: Geneva Press, 2002.

Robinson, William Morrison, Jr. *The Confederate Privateers.* Columbia: University of South Carolina, 1994. Originally published in 1928 by Yale University Press.

Starr, Stephen Z. *The Union Cavalry in the Civil War.* Vol. 2, *The War in the East from Gettysburg to Appomattox, 1863–1865.* Baton Rouge: Louisiana State University Press, 1981.

Tagg, Larry. *The Generals of Gettysburg: The Leaders of America's Greatest Battle.* Boston: Da Capo Press, 2003.

Urwin, Gregory. *Custer Victorious: The Civil War Battles of General George Armstrong Custer.* Lincoln: University of Nebraska Press, 1983.

Wert, Jeffrey D. *A Brotherhood of Valor.* New York: Simon & Schuster, 1999.

———. *Custer: The Controversial Life of George Armstrong Custer.* New York: Simon & Schuster, 1996.

West, Michael P. *30th Battalion Virginia Sharpshooters—The Virginia Regimental Histories Series.* Lynchburg, VA: H.E. Howard Inc., 1995.

Williams, Richard G., Jr. *Lexington, Virginia, and the Civil War.* Charleston, SC: The History Press, 2013.

———. Personal family history, collections and letters. Stuarts Draft, Virginia.

Woodhead, Henry, ed. *Echoes of Glory.* Alexandria, VA: Time-Life Books, 1996.

Index

About the Author

Richard G. Williams Jr. is a southern writer, relic hunter, autodidact and raconteur who specializes in Virginia history and the War Between the States. A former contributor to the *Washington Times'* Civil War column, he has also written for *Homeschooling Today* magazine, *Confederate Veteran* and *Western & Eastern Treasures* magazine and regularly contributes articles about the Civil War and Virginia history to various publications and websites, including Virginia Tech's Virginia Center for Civil War Studies' Sesquicentennial project. He has coproduced two history-related videos: the award-winning *Institute on the Constitution* and *Still Standing: The Stonewall Jackson Story*. His writing and historical research involving the Confederacy earned him the Jefferson Davis Historical Gold Medal from the United Daughters of the Confederacy—the highest honor bestowed on non-members. Williams is a direct descendant of three Confederate soldiers and is a ninth-generation great-grandson of Reverend Roger Williams.

Williams is actively involved in his community, having coached youth basketball, founded a 4H Club and served as a Sunday school teacher for more than thirty-four years. Concerned with preserving Virginia's rich historic heritage, Williams had been a member of the Civil War Preservation Trust and the Museum of the Confederacy. He is currently a member of the Sons of Confederate Veterans and the Archaeological Society of Virginia. He coauthored the text for two of Virginia's historical highway markers and currently serves on the board of trustees for the National Civil War Chaplains Museum in Lynchburg, Virginia, and on the board of directors for the Waynesboro Heritage Foundation in Waynesboro, Virginia. The author of *Christian Business Legends*, *The Maxims of Robert E. Lee for Young Gentlemen*, *Stonewall Jackson: The Black Man's Friend* and *Lexington, Virginia and the Civil War*, Williams lives with his wife and family in Virginia's hallowed and storied Shenandoah Valley. When not working, reading, writing, researching or spending time with his lovely wife or any of his eighteen grandchildren, he can usually be found traipsing through some remote hollow in the Blue Ridge Mountains or some mist-covered battlefield in Virginia, enjoying the company of his ancestors' spirits with a metal detector in his hands, a gleam in his eye and a smile on his face.

www.ingramcontent.com/pod-product-compliance
Lightning Source LLC
Chambersburg PA
CBHW060759100426
42813CB00004B/881